The Amendments
Reshaping the Republic

I am more inclined to define what became of the role for each sovereign state and federal government, rather than just grant undefined, imaginary powers to both federal and state governments.

Federico Lines
States Rights Radio

Copyright © 2026 by Federico Lines, States Rights Radio

All rights reserved. No part of this book may be reproduced in any form or by any means—whether electronic, digital, mechanical, or otherwise—without permission in writing from the publisher, except by a reviewer, who may quote brief passages in a review.

Paperback ISBN: 979-8-218-88980-7

Printed in the United States of America

16 17 18 19 20 21 XXX 9 8 7 6 5 4 3 2 1

CONTENTS

Foreword By Seth Hancock .... *v*

I. The Thirteenth Amendment, 1865 1
    A. Before the Civil War 2
    B. After the Civil War 24
II. The Fourteenth Amendment, 1868 31
    A. Race Relations 38
    B. Immigration and Citizenship Relations 104
    C. Section III Enforcement 130
    D. Marriage Relations 139
    E. Life Relations 156
    F. Identity Relations 178
III. The Fifteenth Amendment, 1870 185
    A. A Right to Vote for All 186
    B. The Right to Vote of 1965 196
    C. Gerrymandering: A tool of Principled Voting ... 211
    D. Women's Right to Vote Small Introduction to the Nineteenth Amendment 221

Bibliography *225*

FOREWORD

Our American republic was built with the glorious common sense of liberty, freedom, and equality. From its Declaration of Independence breaking away from tyranny to form our Constitution's bill of guaranteed rights.

Unfortunately, it took this great republic to fully understand that "we the people" are individuals that need to be respected in order to flourish in this union of sovereign states. The genius of this Constitution is that it can be reshaped for the best of this republic. In this type of reshaping, it is best suited to clarify for the sense of liberty and equality that this nation strived to achieve right after a bloody and disastrous civil war conflict.

I take no pleasure in showing nothing more but discontent for the dark times this nation endured during this bloody conflict between our own countrymen. I have said it multiple times, and so has the author of this book Federico Lines, that this is the only nation on this earth that went to war with itself to be rid of slavery. It could have been resolved by legal and legislative means, but the evils of this two-party system made it possible to further bring this nation into one of the worst divisions of our American republic's history. I personally cast the blame on both sides that began this bloody conflict. As you read this book, even before the war, both sides were too busy to cast themselves to increase the size of the federal government and obtain forceful rights for themselves while denying it others.

As the civil war was approaching its middle horror years, the federal government's executive branch decided to institute an executive order known as the "Emancipation Proclamation." It was an executive order to offer the liberty and freedom to all people that were in slave bondage, a very righteous order that holds the very instances of liberty and equality to our nation's initial striving quality for its Declaration of Independence. But unfortunately, executive orders are not a legal form of legislative remedy, as you may think they are. Even today, I frown upon all executive orders coming out of every single executive administration.

At the very end of this Civil War, finally legal sanity approached our United States Congress and presented this executive order as an amendment to our federal Constitution. As my dear colleague and author of this book has stated, he would have rather seen the abolishment of slavery come about to each individual sovereign state and not by a national directive. But in the end, this is what it took to end it and I guess so be it. The United States Congress then passed this legislation, signed by the president, and then ratified by the sovereign states. This legislation became our **Thirteenth Amendment** to our Constitution abolishing slavery within our union, sovereign states, and its territories.

This nation was on the brink of completely reshaping into a union of full equality and liberty with this amendment. But, of course, as many states, mostly in the south were being repatriated back into the union right after the war, these individuals were not too keen to respect our newly reshaped Constitution with this newly added amendment.

The Amendments

They made it quite difficult to fully embrace this new federal power and give the people that were once in bondage their full freedom. Therefore, many state legislatures across the former states in rebellion established these so-called Apprenticeship laws to still keep in bondage these individuals, but not being called slavery. This was the beginning of an ugly period known as Reconstruction.

As Lines points out, these southern state governments were contradictory before this amendment and being quite contradictory after this amendment passed to our Constitution. This amendment became a federal power that if states fail to follow, the national Congress will initiate legislation to enforce the aspect of this amendment. Reconstruction martial law was established in various southern cities across our union. Federal martial law is not something I or Lines wishes to see, but when an individual or state does not follow through the Constitution, then it is required for the federal government to administer and advise the state government to fully comply with the Constitution.

As many southern states in particular were denying basic rights now granting it to new individuals through our republic, it was evident that the national government had to establish a new form of amendment to clearly reshape and make it known what the true meaning of this American republic means to be filled with liberty and equality.

Even before this union entered a bloody civil conflict, people were not fully understanding what the words "liberty" and "equality" meant in our founding document from different Framers. Yes, our Framers were not perfect, but I believe Lines and I fully understand these words. But we also believed it was up to the heirs of our Framers to reshape this republic to the meaning of those words.

Foreword

Liberty and Equality do not mean dependency from one another. It means we are self-evident to be free and independent from others and from government rulers. Government, both federal and state, are here to ensure our protection against any injustices.

Since many southern state governments failed to grant these two words to many new individuals...then it was up to the federal government to establish it for all. Thus, came the establishment of the **Fourteenth Amendment**. This amendment brought forth a newly defined and reshaping of our American republic of sovereign states. To establish these two words from our constitutional framers to learn that this union is for liberty and equality, the national Congress passed it, the president signed it, and it was ratified by our sovereign states.

This amendment gave not a new meaning to our livelihood for all Americans. But it was a reassuring in reshaping this republic.

I believe, as is described in Lines' book, the federal government should not be the one granting citizenship to all Americans. But if an unconstitutional and racist Chief Justice of the high court, prior to the civil war, did not have these autocratic feelings, we would not have struck down that naturalization enforcement right to the states. We would not be in this predicament that we are enduring now on this federal government power. But we are in this predicament and must treat all persons born here and naturalized as American citizens. The author makes a particularly good point that this amendment is a reassurance of our liberty and equality, and it guarantees our initial bill of rights. There is a due process clause in this amendment but let us not forget that there is also one in the Sixth Amendment. People seem to forget our bill of rights and focus more on this Fourteenth

Amendment. I, along with Lines, do not acknowledge this amendment's right to us, the citizens, as an assurance to the bill of rights. But it is basically a defined tool to enhance federal government protections to us if the state governments fail to protect us from our bill of rights.

Lines does point out that this amendment was not to be used for everything and for the courts to define it for some and deny it for all. In the cause for liberty and equality for all Americans under the law, it is a very much needed protection from all governments. In the sense of what many minority American citizens endured all across our union was detestable. With the unjust and unconstitutional ruling in 1896 labeling a 'Separate but Equal' clause was not what the framers and its heirs wanted to reshape this republic with liberty and equality. This amendment clearly means that all persons who are born within this union or naturalized are citizens and also in respect of the due process system. We live in a due process nation, not in a protective custody nation, as Lines has pointed out many times across his book.

Marriage should be defined by each individual and not by any form of government. But unfortunately, when a state restricts for the individual to enjoy this right…especially an interracial marriage lifestyle, there is federal government protection under this amendment when it considers it a matter of race and, or color, not of sex, or same-sex, or identity issues.

Lines does point out that if the 2015 same-sex marriage supreme court case involved two interracial same-sex couple…there is indeed a Fourteenth Amendment challenge that would be unlike that of the present case involving two white same-sex couple.

Regarding the life issue affecting our republic's meaning of a Fourteenth Amendment challenge, I do differ from the author's point of view. Me, being a Christian, believe in the sanctity of life. Lines believes that the life issue belongs to the individual, and no government, state or federal, can restrict it, prohibit it, or force it upon or against us. My take is that the question of when does life begin is paramount to determining the issue. If life begins at conception, as I believe, then preborn Americans are guaranteed the same rights, not special rights, as the rest of us. I will note, the First Amendment allows us to have disagreements and state our cases, something Lines and I value.

However, both Lines and I understand the Fourteenth was specific to racial issues. That was its intent, and intentions are important. I do believe the unborn deserve the same rights as all Americans, but it would require an amendment.

At this time, the problem that we are facing in properly reshaping our republic is we have failed as a society to really learn our Constitution and its words from its original form to its amendments to correctly reshape our union of sovereign states. And commonsense constitutionalists are at a disadvantage towards constitutionalist dreamers from the left-wing critics and right-wing skeptics.

This is a major point that Lines points out all across this chapter on the Fourteenth Amendment. The Fourteenth protects us from abuses, but they are clearly defined by racial injustices for all Americans, not on the basis on anything else but race or color; black, white, Hispanic, Asian, European, African, Oceania races. All people that wish to enter this union to be a part of it with diversity, equality, and liberty are welcome.

Now that this amendment has come to pass, it has made all persons of different races and colors lawful citizens and non-citizens of our republic of sovereign states. We come to another amendment, granted by the federal government… the right to vote.

The Amendments

Again, because various states, from north, south, central, and pacific regions, were being unjust with the newly made citizens of our republic, they were being denied the proper procedure to participate in our voting community. If the states would have entered into this newly reshaped republic to grant its citizens the right to obtain this privilege to vote, we again would not be in this predicament. I and Lines have agreed that the right to vote should not be a right but a privilege. But here we are, and now we must recognize this right.

The Fifteenth Amendment was then passed by our national Congress, signed by the president, and ratified by the states. One thing Lines points out is that the federal government has given us this right and protection of it, while the states still control their electoral process and standards.

Lines clearly states not to confuse the two or disregard both of these rights. Again, unfortunately various states were indeed infringing on the individual's right to vote by denying them the entry to cast their ballot by way of a poll tax or literacy test. This is indeed a violation of the Fifteenth Amendment and by the way we must ensure a federal government protection through federal legislation. Thus, came the 1965 Voting Rights Act to protect us from being denied our right to vote.

This is the first and only form of federal government protection to protect us from this violation. Lines acknowledges that the federal government has given us this right to vote, and no state can deny us to cast our ballot. But it is up to each state to respect it. But if the individual does cast their vote and it is not properly cast... then it is not fulfilled. It is not denied, because the voter did cast it per their right... but not processed because it did not follow the instructions of the state legislature that passed electoral legislation, per their electoral right.

Lines brings up the perfect example of the 2000 presidential election and especially what happened in the Sunshine state of Florida. I quite agree with him, no voter was denied their right to vote unless they are properly casted their ballot to "punch it through" and not leave any dimple or hanging chad per the state of Florida electoral standard.

A national voting standard by either a conservative (Republican) or liberal (Democrat) party or movement is not what I or Lines are seeking or wanting. We cannot grant or deny the rights of a sovereign state embedded in the electoral clauses. Or also grant or deny it to the individual voter's right embedded in the Fifteenth Amendment.

Gerrymandering is now a new word definition oddly defined by the evils of this two-political party system. Gerrymandering was a tool founded by one of our constitutional framers, Elbridge Gerry. Gerrymandering is a tool of principled politics, not of party politics. What both parties are doing is to deny the voters their right under the Fifteenth Amendment and the state's right under the electoral clauses. They are both on the lust for power and denying our constitution and all rights embedded in it.

* * *

What I got from this book is hopefully what every liberty-loving and equality-loving American from all across our union obtain from this book. That is a sense of knowledge to understand the purpose of these Civil War Amendments, the purpose why they were established to gain the commonsense ideas from our Framers to their heirs and authors of these amendments.

In order to follow our meanings from our framers of these two little words that mean a lot…we must reshape this union until we obtain these rights accordingly from Congress and then enforced by either the federal government executive branch or the state governments, and then appropriately interpreted by our courts.

I, as well as Lines, find these three amendments more meaningful to reflect and resemble our framers' ideas than the two unprincipled amendments that were established in 1913. These two amendments adopted no constitutional founding meaning. While these three amendments have more constitutional sense than the Sixteenth and Seventeenth Amendments, I also recommend the author's second book, "The Road to Liberty: Bringing an End to the Unprincipled 16th and 17th Amendments." I strongly recommend this book to really learn about these liberty and equality amendments.

        Seth Hancock
        Journalist
        Seth Hancock Reports
        (https://sethhancock.substack.com/)

I. The Thirteenth Amendment, 1865

Section I, Neither slavery nor involuntary servitude, except as a punishment for crime whereof the party shall have been duly convicted, shall exist within the United States, or any place subject to their jurisdiction.

Section II, Congress shall have power to enforce this article by appropriate legislation.

A. Before the Civil War

This republic unfortunately has a huge blood stain in our American political history and history. This blood stain commenced when this land was a British colonial territory to the entrance of the American civil war. It is known as slavery. America was one of the last nations to end this issue. This issue was not fully resolved by legal legislative means, but by war means.

As you have read in my three books on American federalism is that I do not want to push any national legislative directives onto the sovereign states and its people. When it is a violation of human and civilian rights, then unfortunately a national legislative directive is the only way to solve this situation. Yes, slavery was evil on both accounts but as the constitutional framers, all stated that they abhorred it, but that they did not have any speedy remedy to end this situation.

I believe that the framers of our republic, all wanted to end the blood stain known as slavery but in the unity and spirit of federalism. But unfortunately, the individuals that followed the framers denied the rules of federalism and the sovereign and individual retainment of our rights for the various states and people.

"I go on the ground that this Constitution was made by the States; that it is a federal union of the States, in which the several States still retain their sovereignty."

(Against the Force Bill by John C. Calhoun, 15th & 16th February, 1833).

The Amendments

I believe the early words from the gentleman of South Carolina brought some clarity to what the framers were trying to envision for our republic. In working together to make this nation, a more perfect union of sovereign states, America would be the nation that other foreign nations would admire. That this young nation brought a sense of individual liberty and inspiration to future prospect of nations. Slavery was indeed an abomination that needed to enter extinction. There is no debate about it, but the way various legislators, after the framers came about discussing the issue was an insult to our constitution writers.

The "era of good feelings" of James Monroe, our last framer to serve as our chief executive came to an end. This brought in new blood of individuals. We always need young and new individuals to enter the realm of politics. But as these new individuals enter the halls of politics and government, they must enter with the idea of constitutional federalism principles.

Again, unfortunately, for many new young individuals who enter the halls of government with not a sense of federalism, but a sense of authoritarianism. This type of sense that this union fought it in 1776 and to this day continues to battle with it.

Even before the war and the passage of the Thirteenth Amendment that helped reshape this nation to a new sense of liberty. We were seeing various (sovereign) states started to show some feelings of being dependent off the national government. Whether they used the national Congress to institute obscure constitutional opinions or affirmed by a pretentious high court.

Even though there was a federal ban on the importation on the slave trade, sovereign states were still using that trade.

I could argue that America before the unfortunate civil war conflict, this union was becoming an early version of

I. The Thirteenth Amendment, 1865

a dependent nation. The cases of *McCollough v. Maryland*, 1819; *Cohens v. Virginia*, 1820; *Gibbons v. Ogden*, 1824. These court cases started to make these sovereign states into the realm of dependency.

"The Constitution was formed for all the States; and Congress was to have power to regulate commerce." (The Great Speeches and Orations of Daniel Webster, With an Essay on Daniel Webster as a Master of English Style by Edwin P. Whipple, Daniel Webster. The Case of Gibbons and Ogden in the Supreme Court of the United States, February term, 1824, page 118).

"It should be repeated, that the words used in the Constitution, "to regulate commerce," are so general and extensive, that they may be construed to cover a vast field of legislation, part of which has always been occupied by State laws; and therefore the words must have a reasonable construction, and the power should be considered exclusively vested in Congress so far, and so far only, as the nature of the power requires." (The Great Speeches and Orations of Daniel Webster, With an Essay on Daniel Webster as a Master of English Style by Edwin P. Whipple, Daniel Webster. The Case of Gibbons and Ogden in the Supreme Court of the United States, February term, 1824, page 117).

With this way of thinking of some individuals in the past and future, it is no reason; we are to believe that "We the States" need the federal government rather than "The Federal Government" needs the States. It is sad that even in those earlier times of our American republic, there was a distinct belief of central government dependency and unwanted privilege.

"It declares that Congress ought to possess the sole and exclusive power of regulating trade, as well, with foreign nations as between the States." (The Great Speeches and Orations of Daniel Webster, With an Essay on Daniel Webster as a Master of English Style by Edwin P. Whipple, Daniel Webster. The Case of Gibbons and Ogden in the Supreme Court of the United States, February term, 1824, page 117).

The Amendments

Regulating trade is one thing and enforcing trade is another. Another word for "regulating" is supervising or administering. It was never in the best interest of most of the Framers to grant Congress the right to possess the power of enforcing trade. Even with foreign nations, the Constitution is not asking for the States to conduct diplomatic meetings with foreign nations. The Constitution is asking for the States to enforce the clause and conduct themselves in a business cordial atmosphere while enforcing trade with other sister States, foreign nations, and native Indian tribes.

The national Congress has the power to regulate commerce, not to enforce commerce. In other words, they are here to administer commerce. The commerce relations are left to the States and their individuals to enforce.

The federal government was never to be considered the official law-enforcer of the commercial trade among the States. Within the international trade among the different nations, yes, it is the power of the national government's national State Department. Sadly, in the first years of this new republic, there was a rise of centrist-authoritarians in control of Congress.

"In the discussion in the New York courts, no small reliance was placed on the law of that State prohibiting the importation of slaves, as an example of a commercial regulation enacted by state authority. That law may or may not be constitutional and valid. It has been referred to generally, but its particular provisions have not been stated. When they are more clearly seen, its character may be better determined." (The Great Speeches and Orations of Daniel Webster, With an Essay on Daniel Webster as a Master of English Style by Edwin P. Whipple, Daniel Webster. The Case of Gibbons and Ogden in the Supreme Court of the United States, February term, 1824, page 119).

I. The Thirteenth Amendment, 1865

Even though, the national Congress had voted to ban the United States government from the international slave trade. The United States government did not have any right to ban it for the states themselves. It is a policy for the sovereign states themselves to decide. If a sovereign state wants to make a law to themselves to ban the importation of the international slave trade, then it is in my humble constitutional opinion to the rules of federalism. That other states will see this and follow suit to make this a more workable and perfect union of sovereign states.

If a very profitable and commercial state like New York sees fit to not join and ban the international slave trade. Then it will create an economic and political hardships for those states that continue to operate in the slave trade and be able to conduct business. This was one of the reasons that Jefferson said that he did not have a centrist idea to be rid of slavery, but he did share his views that constructed this union under the idea of federalism.

With individuals that supported the *Gibbons v. Ogden* decision like Daniel Webster, he truly did not understand the framers that built this republic. Individuals like Webster wanted the central government known as the federal government to dictate these policies of commerce and trade, and that includes the slave importation.

After the unfortunate Marshall court had these authoritarian-centrist rulings against the sovereign rights of a state. Then came the Taney court and that truly set the precedence of federal government precedence over a state sovereign precedence. A precedence set by greedy special interests over constitutional interests.

It is my humble constitutional opinion that if the federal government did not meddle in the affairs of the states. We would have seen a different outcome come in the 1850's and later in 1865. But it is quite ill-fated that our first generations of statesmen after our framers did not quite entail the pride of federalism that built this republic.

That first generation of statesmen did forego an unfortunate and unprecedented powers to the general government that we are suffering today. I still say that if New York would have been allowed to ban the importation of the international slave trade...that idea would have welcomed a new wave of economic prosperity.

Since the high court began banning a sovereign state to ban this sort of trade. It let the other states with existing slave laws continue to be hardships, not for economic times but for human and citizenship right violations. The battle for expansion for new territories out in the west, so-called "Manifest Destiny," was being a problem between the northern and southern states. Southern and northern legislators started to now look further into their special interests and throw out the Constitution. The 1820 Missouri Compromise should not have taken a precedence, but again the *Gibbons* decision let it come to play. Missouri entered as a slave state, while Maine entered as a free state. Then came the Compromise of 1850, a deep, awful, and unconstitutional compromise ever came to a discussion.

The Fugitive Slave law of 1850 was modeled after the Fugitive Slave law of 1793 with the intent to enforce article IV, section II, clause III:

> "No person held to service or Labour in one State, under the Laws thereof, escaping into another, shall, in Consequence of any Law or Regulation therein, be discharged from such Service or Labour, but shall be delivered up on Claim of the Party to whom such Service or Labour may be due."

I. The Thirteenth Amendment, 1865

The term of slavery was not within the Constitution. But many legislators from southern states demanded to adapt these fugitive laws to capture a slave or indentured servants, who escaped their proprietor. These federal laws granting the federal government to place funds and aid towards these states with slave laws…became an act of dependency. A type of act that was never granted to the general government of the United States before or after the adoption of the 1787 Constitution.

Roger Sherman of Connecticut objected of this act and stated, "that this provision would oblige the Executive of the State to do it at public expense."

It is not only the state government to issue public funds at their expense. But this began the use of federal government public funds and aid into the states without any use of state government funds. Welcome to the era of dependency.

In 1842, a mixture of principles and feelings ruling decree came about in the high court. "Federal law is superior to state law, but states are not required to use their resources to enforce federal law," *Prigg v. Pennsylvania*, 1842, Associate Justice Joseph Story. The Prigg decision has it half-wrong and a damage to the rules of federalism of our American union of sovereign states.

Federal law IS NOT superior to state law, AND states are indeed not required or demanded to use their resources to enforce federal law. We have seen uncontrollable power grabs by the federal government even before 1842 and way after 1842.

To decide the slavery question, we surely did not need to involve the likes of the General Government of the United States' institutions. It should have been decided by a majority of the sovereign states. If all decided to begin to outlaw the slave trade and slavery itself, then this nation would not have endured the tragic bloodbath of a civil war.

The 1850 Fugitive Slave law did just that and opened a full can of funds and aid into states where they sought to defy it. Within that can of funds and aid…gave the southern states a pedestal of dependency and privilege that it did not exist since the constitutional adoption, a very sickening display, that we still see today.

As the first Framers' heirs were in mind, Henry Clay (1777-1852) of Kentucky, John C. Calhoun (1782-1850) of South Carolina, and Daniel Webster (1782-1852) of New Hampshire were great statesmen that tried somewhat to live up to the framer's republic standards. Enter Judah P. Benjamin (1811-1884) of Louisiana, Stephen A. Douglas (1793-1863) of Illinois, and Sam Houston (1813-1861) of Texas. All men of different ideals but in the end all on the basic principle of the constitution and federalism.

"All America acknowledges the existence of slavery to be an evil, which it deprives the slave of the best gift of heaven, in the end injures the master too, by laying waste his lands, enabling him to live indolently, and thus contracting all the vices generated by a state of idleness. If it be this enormous evil, the sooner we attempt its destruction the better." Henry Clay.

"Judah P. Benjamin, on the other hand, believed that there were constitutional problems in building a transcontinental railroad without the consent of the states, and other southerners opposed it as a device to strengthen the political power of the North. But Davis's response answer to construct the railroad before the territories became states. While he was narrow on interpreting the Constitution as to states' rights, Davis was always expansionist in foreign policy, advocating the extension of Texas to the Rio Grande and the acquisition

I. The Thirteenth Amendment, 1865

of Cuba, as well as the building of the railroad to the West."
(Judah P. Benjamin, The Jewish Confederate, Eli N. Evans, The Free Press, a division of MacMillan, Inc., pp. 88, 1988).

Judah P. Benjamin, a distinct voice for federalism but still appealing to a southern special interest instead of a constitutional interest. While Davis never showed an inch of constitutional interest but to the expansion of his own interests in the sense of specialty to the expansion of slavery.

"The Constitution was a 'compact' among equals. Take away this league of love, convert it into a bond of distrust of suspicion, or of hate; and the entire fabric which is held together by that cement will crumble to the earth, and rest scattered in dishonest fragments upon the ground," stated Judah P. Benjamin on the national senate floor. (Judah P. Benjamin, The Jewish Confederate, Eli N. Evans, The Free Press, a division of MacMillan, Inc., pp. 90, 1988).

I will tend to agree and disagree with the fine gentleman of Louisiana. The Constitution is indeed a compact of equals. But when you have special interests clouding the Constitution's equality judgment, you bring in privilege and not equality. We saw this bond of distrust of suspicion while creating an Imperial Congress, rather than a republican Congress with the adoption of the Fugitive Slave Law.

Jefferson Davis, you know him as the first and only president to the failed nation of the Confederate States of America. He served as Secretary of War during President Pierce's presidency. Neo-confederates across this land sing praises to this man, but not me. Here is a man that never respected the rules of federalism or the retainment of the state sovereign rights of the rest of the states.

"The Secretary of War extended his interests beyond military affairs; his influence over a weak president grew so strong that a Mississippi newspaper called him "the de-facto president" and the great Mogul. Davis persuaded Pierce to support the Kansas-Nebraska bill in 1854, which broke up the Compromise of 1850, allowing slavery in the territories." (Judah P. Benjamin, The Jewish Confederate, Eli N. Evans, The Free Press, a division of MacMillan, Inc., pp. 86, 1988).

There you see the power-hungry stature of Jefferson Davis. Trying to initiate military aid and support to pursue a special interest rather than a constitutional interest. A piece of land not acquired by a sovereign state is the distinct property of the federal government. It is a property controlled by the national Congress, not by any state legislature or composed unity of state legislatures.

"Nothing, therefore, as it seems to me, can be clearer, than that the States making the cession expected Congress to exercise over the District precisely that power, and neither more nor less, which the Constitution had conferred upon it. I do not know how the provision, or the intention, either of the Constitution in granting the power, or of the States in making the cession, could be expressed in a manner more absolutely free from all doubt or ambiguity." (Slavery in the District of Columbia. Remarks made in the Senate of the United States, on the 10th of January 1838, upon a resolution moved by Mr. Clay as a substitute for the resolution offered by Mr. Calhoun on the subject of slavery in the District of Columbia, page 365).

"I see, therefore, nothing in the act of cession, and nothing in the Constitution, and nothing in the history of this transaction, and nothing in any other transaction upon the authority of Congress." (Slavery in the District of Columbia. Remarks made in the Senate of the United States, on the 10th of January 1838, upon a resolution moved by Mr. Clay as a substitute for the resolution offered by Mr. Calhoun on the subject of slavery in the District of Columbia, page 365).

"The honorable member of Kentucky asks the Senate to suppose the opposite case; to suppose that the seat of government had been fixed in a free State, Pennsylvania,

I. The Thirteenth Amendment, 1865

for example; and that Congress had attempted to establish slavery in a district over which, as here, it had thus exclusive legislation. He asks whether, in that case, Congress could establish slavery in such a place." (Slavery in the District of Columbia. Remarks made in the Senate of the United States, on the 10th of January 1838, upon a resolution moved by Mr. Clay as a substitute for the resolution offered by Mr. Calhoun on the subject of slavery in the District of Columbia, page 365).

Of all the three first Framers' heirs, I would believe that Mr. Henry Clay was the closest to the Framer's ideals of our American republic.

Daniel Webster or John C. Calhoun did not come close to those constitutionalism ideals, because they both lacked to what Clay had... constitutional federalism.

It does not matter where the national governing body sat. In an area where slavery was permitted, or slavery that was prohibited. The authority of controlling the territories that have not been admitted as a sovereign state into this union belong upon the authority of Congress. Henry Clay, a Virginian-born but represented the hills of Kentucky understood the rules of federalism that governed this republic.

The terminology of the "rules of federalism" was a first term to be known in the late of the eighteenth century. It was a new term to describe the form of governing bodies of this new republic installed after its victorious victory to break away from the ancient monarchial tyrannies of Europe.

A clear definition of the rules of federalism is to distinct the powers of a centralized authority and individual and/or sovereign state authority.

The national government can dictate decrees onto federal properties and territories, but never onto and against the sovereign states. For Congress to install what decrees for the state's lives and its citizens, is an authoritarian point of view and for a member of the executive branch to try

The Amendments

to persuade to be more directed on a position of a state is abhorrently tyrannical.

"An Act to amend, and supplementary to, the Act entitled "An Act respecting Fugitives from Justice, and Persons escaping from their Service of their Masters," approved February twelfth, one-thousand seven hundred and ninety-three."

California entered as a free state, and the second dependent act from the federal government was established. The Fugitive Slave law was set as a general government directive onto and against the states.

After 1850 was a change in the presidency and a change in leadership to continue the legacy of the constitutional framers. With this new leadership they had to endure the oppressive central authority congressional act of the Fugitive Slave law.

Abolitionists indeed opposed this law with a passion, while southerner-slavers supported it. Still sovereign states had a duty to retain their sovereignty and declare this law null and void and refuse to cooperate with federal union officials.

And we had various states with anti-slavery policies resist these measures. These forms of resistance, not rebellion, appeared from various northern states.

The sovereign state of Wisconsin, its high court, was the only high court that declared this usurper federal law unconstitutional. This case involved a fugitive slave by name of Joshua Glover and an abolitionist by the name of Sherman Booth.

If the individual Sherman Booth presented his case onto the Wisconsin state legislature. Then the legislature itself would have presented this nullification act against this federal law instead of the Wisconsin high court…I think we would have seen a different outcome. People using the courts for

I. The Thirteenth Amendment, 1865

their personal justice is not the correct way to do it. And of course, the esteemed high court of this land overruled this case and shut down the state sovereign doctrine, not only for the northern states but for all states.

"it was felt by the statesmen who framed the Constitution and by the people who adopted it that it was necessary that many rights of sovereignty which the States then possessed should be ceded to the General Government, and that, in the sphere of action assigned to it, it should be supreme, and strong enough to execute its own laws by its own tribunals, without interruption from a State or from State authorities."
(Chief Justice Roger Taney, Ableman v. Booth, 1859).

"...that many rights of sovereignty which the States then possessed should be *ceded* to the General Government." *Ceded* to the General Government?! The arrogant gall of this individual that sat as the chief justice to the high court of the land. It was no surprise of mine that Chief Justice Taney had such arrogance as he decreed this opinion, appointed by the first arrogant president in our republic's history, Andrew Jackson. With this type of constitutional opinion given by a member of the federal government began to seal the fate to what our framers tried to envision for our republic. With this sealed tragic fate, truly started a full era of federal dependency that we are seeing today with other issues.

After this law passed, the first state to nullify and refuse to cooperate was the state of Vermont. This law in Vermont fully made the federal act unenforceable across the border of Vermont. President Millard Fillmore threatened this state with military action to enforce the said act. I would say that the U.S. Colonel Robert E. Lee famous quote, just before the outbreak of the civil war is well suited to criticize President Fillmore. "My country, Mr. Blair, I never thought I'd see the day when a President of the United States would raise an army to invade his own county."

Of course, from southern congressional delegates to southern public officials were crying that various states were not obeying an unjust and unconstitutional law. Virginia governor John B. Floyd made a statement that nullification could move the various southern states into secession. Governor Floyd was just seeking federal funds to pour into his beloved commonwealth for his own personal special interest agenda and disregard for the republic's constitutional agenda. This sort of action is like today's red state's congressional delegations and public officials crying that various blue states are not enforcing the so-called federal immigration laws and requesting federal assistance to invade these sovereign states.

It is not surprising to see various southern states claim dependency and funds to the federal government. Even today's southern congressional delegations are more dependent now than what they were back in 1850.

A whole bunch of sovereign states introduced and passed nullification and liberty laws against this federal act. States like Michigan, Connecticut, Massachusetts, Maine, New Hampshire, Ohio, Pennsylvania, and Wisconsin were states that championed the rules of federalism and individual state sovereignty.

A state is not here to create an alliance with the central government. And all Americans should understand in order to create and form this almost perfect union of sovereign states.

The decision of *Dred Scott v. Sanford*, 1857 did not help the cause of federalism and entered a realm of central government autocracy.

I. The Thirteenth Amendment, 1865

1. Persons of African descent cannot be and were never intended to be citizens under the U.S. Constitution. Plaintiff is without standing to file a suit.
2. The Property Clause is applicable only to lands possessed at the time of the Constitution's ratification (1787). As such, Congress cannot ban slavery in the territories. The Missouri Compromise is unconstitutional.
3. The Due Process Clause of the Fifth Amendment prohibits the federal government from freeing slaves brought into federal territories.

This decision was an upset to the constitutional framers and those who believe in our American rules of federalism way of life. This decision is full of contradictions and filled with the utmost hypocrisy.

1. So, a person of Irish, German, Scottish, English, Italian nationality entering this land, have more rights than an individual of African descent that has been born in this country? It is blatantly filled with ignorance and racism to the absolute extreme.
2. The second holding is an absolute disgrace to the majority of the justices' special interest and not to the Constitution. If the Missouri Compromise was to be an unconstitutional piece of action, then the states of Missouri and Maine would become territories. Missouri was a slave state, while Maine was a free state. I seriously doubt that the citizens of Maine and their neighbors would accept and allow slavery among its territories.
3. The court is dictating what policy can be found and dictated by the federal government and/or a sovereign state. It is not in the best interest of the court to legislate or decree a law or order. It is in their best interest of the court to interpret the legislation or order.

The Amendments

This decision truly was one of the deciding factors that led us to the civil war and later the adoption of the three Amendments. If the high court did not hold such special interests to their farms, and rather to the Constitution. I would not be inclined to point the fingers at this court for igniting the civil war.

The *Ableman v. Booth*, 1859 decision was an attack on our state and individual sovereign power. But the *Dred Scott v. Sanford*, 1857 decision was an attack on basic human rights, which applies within the Constitution on individual liberty. The Constitution has no pro-slavery or anti-slavery clause, and it is plain common sense that all those individuals, either natural-born or naturalized residing in our union are citizens and adopted by their respective state.

If you note in the Bill of Rights, the national government has no rights embedded onto itself. All rights embedded in the Bill of Rights are toward the individual and state. Of course, as arrogant as individuals in power from the federal government, they will take what is not theirs and claim it as their own.

I am more interested to analyze the political history that regrettably led us to a very unpleasant civil war than the history of the war itself. I am more incline to define what became of the role for each sovereign state and federal government, rather than just grant undefined, imaginary powers to both federal and state powers to clearly analyze the rules of federalism when these amendments were adopted and ratified into our Constitution.

"And now to you, Mr. President, and to my brother Senators, on all sides of this Chamber, I bid a respectful farewell; with many of those from whom I have been radically separated in political sentiment, my personal relations have been kindly and have inspired me with a respect and esteem from the Southern states, I part as men part from

I. The Thirteenth Amendment, 1865

brothers on the eve of a temporary absence, with a cordial pressure of the hand and smiling assurance of sweet intercourse around the family hearth. But to you, noble and generous friends, who, born beneath other skies, possess hearts that beat sympathy with ours...to you, on our behalf have bared your breast to the fierce beatings of the storm... in your devotion to constitutional liberty; to you, who made our cause your cause and from many of whom I part forever... one priceless treasure is yours—the assurance that an entire people honor your names, and hold them in grateful and affectionate memory... When, in after days, the story of the present shall be written; when history shall have passed her stern sentence on the erring men who have driven their unoffending brethren from the shelter of their common home... your children shall hear repeated the familiar tale... and they will glory in their lineage from men of spirit as generous and of patriotism as high hearted as ever illustrated or adorned the American Senate." "On January 26, 1861, Louisiana seceded from the union and on February 4 Benjamin and Slidell officially withdrew from their seats in the Senate." (Judah P. Benjamin, The Jewish Confederate, Eli N. Evans, The Free Press, a division of MacMillan, Inc., pp. 110-111, 1988).

"Judah P. Benjamin was part of the small band of moderates who tried to hold the union together but were not able to compromise on slavery." (Judah P. Benjamin, The Jewish Confederate, Eli N. Evans, The Free Press, a division of MacMillan, Inc., pp. 112, 1988).

"The Senate was hushed in stillness," wrote Senator Bragg of North Carolina, "so that every word in his soft but distinct utterance fell clearly upon the ears of his hearers." Bragg reported that both Benjamin and Slidell shed tears, and that he shook their hands, "too full to say the word." (Judah P. Benjamin, The Jewish Confederate, Eli N. Evans, The Free Press, a division of MacMillan, Inc., pp. 111, 1988).

The Amendments

Exiting Senator Benjamin's farewell speech was inspiring to some but not to those who hold federalism and the Constitution close to their principled hearts. Yes, Benjamin was a moderate-minded person of the Democratic party of those days, but he still contained special interests clouding his constitutional interests.

I would have pondered this idea to these constitutional framers and to the first framers' heirs of this republic. Imagine if this national Congress was built with a proportional multi-party representation system. Instead of a two-party system. A two-party system would cling more into political partisanship chaos. While a multi-political party or movement system would create more reaching across the aisle to bring good, hearty, and respectful agreements to better reshape our American republic. Prior to the American civil war and during the war itself, the debate was heavily debated, filled with unwanted political partisan hack talk. The Democratic party screaming to preserve the union with the current slave-labor system and expansion of it, while the Republican party seeking to preserve the union with the abolishment of slavery and the expansion of it. Actually, we saw a break-out of movements come out of both of these political party systems.

The break-out was mostly from the Democratic party from various different sanctions trying to persuade secession and others trying to avoid it. The candidate from the Democratic party, Stephen A. Douglas, even though he wanted to preserve and extend slavery, he was a staunch unionist. But, unfortunately, the Democratic party had a major split to secede and continue the slave-labor system under candidate John C. Breckenridge. While the Constitutional Union Party refused to join the two umbrella parties but really showed no difference to the Republican or Democratic parties.

I. The Thirteenth Amendment, 1865

These parties/movements split, but just made a drastic split but still remain with the same ideas, and nothing new brought forth to the negotiating table. It was not truly a multiple party proportional system.

Because of this unfortunate system, even today, this continuing two party system is creating more divisions than unifying a nation under its constitutional rule. I strongly believe that a multiple party proportional representative system, this union of sovereign states would have been more successful to fully continue the rules of federalism than a useless, partisanship of two political parties. If people like Judah Benjamin and Sam Houston had a larger following of moderate democratic views and really broke-off from the Democratic party, a silly civil war conflict could have been avoided. But neither party had a true break-out from either them, to really show debate and discussions to preserve the union without the existence of slavery and the expansion of it.

Unfortunately, these moderate and conservative minds of those dangerous times for our republic and later during the Confederacy brought nothing but chaos and disorder to our true form of our American federalism republic of sovereign states. We truly wonder of this possible alternative point of history route that this union would have taken.

* * *

We begin with the first battle of the political civil war battle that brought the end of slavery as a national whole.

That on September 22, 1862, President Abraham Lincoln signed the initial Emancipation Proclamation or in other words, Executive Order 95, to free the enslaved people from all realms of this union.

The Amendments

"That on the first day of January, in the year of our Lord, one-thousand and sixty-three, all persons held as slaves within any State or designated part of a State, the people whereof shall then be in rebellion against the United States, shall be then, thenceforward, and forever free."

This was beginning that this union of sovereign states enter world of freedom and liberty for all without racism and discrimination. Unfortunately, various constitutional legal scholars, not bias to a northern or southern point of view. Even though, the war had achieved a northern (federal government) union victory, the executive order placed by Lincoln would soon cease to disappear. As we all know that executive orders are not legislation to be added into our Constitution to protect the rights of all citizens.

Lincoln knew that his executive order would be tossed out like a old newspaper because it holds no true constitutional weight...and the only way to hold this form of liberty was to introduce it to Congress as a way of a constitutional amendment.

The Constitution is an original document in a living union, and thus abled to be amended and changed. The ability to change it and remaining its principle status of its framers' vision. I believe that adding the Thirteenth Amendment to our Constitution does not make it an unprincipled one but a principled one. It brings all citizens of all walks of life as a step for liberty and towards a step of citizenship and citizen participation.

The battle in accepting the Thirteenth was as difficult as the Battle of Gettysburg. The national Senate, on April 8, 1864, by a vote of thirty-eight to six passed the amendment legislation.

I. The Thirteenth Amendment, 1865

The lonely two senators casting a negative vote were Senators Benjamin F. Harding and James Nesmith, both of Oregon. It appears that Oregon was wishing it would return to a federal territory status under the natural nature of dependency off the federal government.

The legislation reached the national house just before the 1864 elections but fell short of thirteen votes. There were no southern representatives represented in the Congress, so the bill did not fail immensely.

Ohio Democrat Chilton A. White gave a chilling and unflattering warning that the abolition of slavery would leave the freed slaves into citizenship status. A type of warning of those that contain racist sentiments that truly does not belong in the halls of Congress. People of races, creed, and different nationalities are all welcome to this union and subject to the laws of that sovereign state. But because we had to introduce these amendments in the national government. The state sovereign right and sentiment of federalism began to lose its liberty aroma it once had in 1776.

I do not question or reject this amendment or the two following amendments. I question and reject the very thought of disgust by individuals that undermined and failed to comprehend to understand the new reshaping applications to the rules of federalism.

On January 31, 1865, the national house speaker called for another vote to the abolition of slavery legislation. This time, all members in support of this amendment were confident that it was going to pass. The legislation that became the Thirteenth Amendment finally sounded the voice of liberty with a vote of one-hundred and nineteenth to fifty-six.

A civil war was going to decide the fate of this union and slavery. But in the end, it was fatefully decided like other nations decided... the will of a legislative directive, a national directive though. I wished it did not turn to be this route but when you have selfish, free-loathing, arrogant, and filled with special interest individuals over the Constitution, I support the Constitution's amending power to an extent. The rules of federalism that once existed began to fade away because of constitutional federalism ignorance that ran ramped it during Reconstruction and the segregation era. But I always say that these three amendments became part of this constitutional compact. New framers to our republic have reshaped this republic for a new era of human rights and citizen rights. It is now to read and clearly define the powers of all entities and not offer any false narrative to the new effect that has reshaped this republic.

B. After the Civil War

After the Thirteenth Amendment passed the national Congress amid of the final months of the civil war. It was time to bring unity and liberty all around this union of sovereign states with newly enumerated powers of the federal government. But state sovereignty rights and individual rights should have never been a target to this newly added power of the central government. This federal amendment now went to the various states for ratification into the Constitution.

But unfortunately, for the current states in rebellion, news had not reached of this constitutional amendment. Also, the type of this news source information was still not perfected to reach thousands of citizens and they were still relying on the Wells Fargo coach hands and United States Pony Express systems.

The amendment was passed on the first of the year in 1865, but regrettably the news did not reach white citizens and the newly freed black citizens till the mid-of 1865.

W.E.B Dubois stated in 1935, "Slavery was not abolished even after the Thirteenth Amendment. There were four million freedmen and most of them on the same plantation, doing the same work they did before emancipation except as their work had been interrupted and changed by the upheaval of war."

The Amendments

People should recognize January 31, 1865 as the official day that ended slavery. Again, regrettably, people in recent days recognized the day, Juneteenth: June 19, 1865. As the day that ended slavery. I guess Juneteenth sounds better for marketing purposes than Januaryteenth.

People, as constitutional framer Roger Sherman once noted that the people tend to be held liable and misled from information.

I am not worried about one day that false historians are noting that ended slavery. I am worried for the upcoming days that this nation had to endure that the newly repatriated states in the southern region that even though they ratified this amendment...decided to contradict federal constitutional law.

Enter the "great" state of Mississippi: The Magnolia State, to be one of the first states to contradict this amendment. Not only did this state restrict the newly made black citizens to their second amendment right. But what troubles me and would like to discuss is the reinstated state legislatures of the southern states, including Mississippi established "Apprenticeship Laws."

Mississippi and various southern states entered black racist codes into state laws to restrict blacks from an equal form of life and punish sympathetic white citizens on a crusade for equality under law.

> "That all freedmen, free negroes and mulattoes in this State, over the age of eighteen years, found on the second Monday in January, 1866, or thereafter, without lawful employment or business, or found unlawfully assembling themselves together, either in the day or night time, and all white persons so assembling themselves with freedmen, free

I. The Thirteenth Amendment, 1865

negroes or mulattoes, or usually associating with freedmen, free negroes or mulattoes, on terms of equality, living in adultery or fornication with a freed woman, free negro or mulatto, shall be deemed vagrants, and of conviction thereof shall be fined in a sum not exceeding, in the case of a freedman, free negro or mulatto, fifty dollars, and a white man two hundred dollars, and imprisoned, at the discretion of the court, the free negro not exceeding ten days, and the white man not exceeding six months."

This is the problem that came after the civil war. The war itself was perpetrated by a southern aristocracy. But after the war and the individuals that heavily invested into this failed venture known as the Confederate States of America went bankrupt. Let us all remember that the ones that had some finances that refuse to give it to the union federal government escaped to the southern nation of Brazil and settled in a small village that is known today as Americana, Brazil.

After this aristocracy was removed from the southern way of life. The only ones left to govern these newly repatriated states were the common soldiery and low-level junior military officers of a failed southern army. They indeed have a chip on their shoulder because they, in my opinion, were chess pawns to the King and Queen of a Confederacy chess game. So, these bitter white under-privileged individuals did what they did for vengeance. To punish the old South, and to punish the newly freed American individuals.

"If any apprentice shall leave without consent "said master may pursue and recapture the apprentice and bring him

The Amendments

before any justice of the peace whose duty it shall be to remand said apprentice to the service of his or her master."

Prior to the union military occupation in the various southern states, I understand in where martial law applied to these states. Because the various state legislatures were contradicting the federal constitution. They were passing laws still affecting the livelihood and work life of these individuals.

Even though, the newly freed citizens were no longer considered slaves. Yet, they were still being treated as such with such little pay and no accommodations to their livelihood and liberty.

States like South Carolina, and Mississippi, especially, targeted freedmen and freedwomen to be subject of new punishable state laws. Punishable state laws to bring them back to the cotton fields with little pay and no accommodations.

"Mississippi Black Code, 1866: Article IV—Penal Code: Section I. Be it enacted by the legislature of the State of Mississippi, that no freedman, free negro, or mulatto not in the military service of the United States government, and not licensed so to do by the board of police of his or her county, shall keep or carry firearms of any kind, or ammunition, dirk, or Bowie knife; and, on conviction thereof in the county court, shall be punished by fine, no exceeding $10, and pay the costs of such proceedings, and all such arms or any ammunition shall be forfeited to the informer; and it shall be the duty of every civil and military officer to arrest any freedman, free negro, or mulatto found with any such arms or ammunition, and cause him or her to be committed for trial in default of bail…

Section III: Be further enacted enacted, that if any white person shall sell, lend, or give any freedman, negro, or mulatto any firearms, dirk, or Bowie knife, or ammunition, or any

I. The Thirteenth Amendment, 1865

spiritous or intoxicating liquors, such person or persons so offending, upon conviction thereof in the county court of his or her county, shall be fined not exceeding $50, and may be imprisoned, at the discretion of the court, not exceeding thirty days..." (Race & Liberty in America, The Essential Reader, Edited by Jonathan Bean, The Independent Institute, The University Press of Kentucky, 2009, pp. 64).

Due to these unfortunate legislative directives in states like in Mississippi, northern public sentiment started to worry that their battle that ended in slavery would have died with no sense of purpose. The national Congress passed the 1866 Civil Rights Act and that brought an end to all southern black codes and achieving the freedmen male and female individuals with deserving fundamental rights, and not de facto slave workers. With congressional enforcement of the amendment, began the reign of terror in the south with the rise of the racist organization known as the Ku Klux Klan.

The national Congress initiated to create military districts under martial law and passed legislation to arrest, prosecute, and punish members of the Ku Klux Klan that did any harm to the many freedmen individuals exercising their rights as promised to them.

The Thirteenth Amendment was easy to enforce by congressional acts because the language was quite clear. The form of slavery and involuntary servitude ceased to be ended in our republic. But unfortunately, the civil war continued because there were individuals not understanding the new constitution's amendment. They either did not understand it or failed to comprehend that the war was lost, and they unfortunately had to adapt to the republic's new form of constitutional governance.

Fortunately, with this new constitutional governance led to new legality and equality forms of amendments that continued and continue to shape our republic as to bring equality to our American individual person. These are newly added and enumerated powers of the federal government that brought a new form of rights, civil rights. And to preserve our rules of federalism is that sovereign states must abide these constitutional compact's new laws.

This chapter discusses the extinction of slavery from the realms of our union of sovereign states. Yes, by a national amendment from our nation's Congress. If the states were not willing to accept each other's respect for their sovereignty. Then it was necessary and proper for the national government to adopt an amendment to prohibit slavery and involuntary servitude. I do not hardly quote from a ruling from Chief Justice John Marshall, but in this case, I will gladly quote from him to point out the cruelty of slavery. I will make my point clear from the words of Chief Justice Marshall of "necessary and proper" to abolish the form of labor known as slavery.

Hence, the next chapter is to discuss the way the federal government initiated the amendment that made all persons, whether legal or not legal equal under law without the threat of intimidation, discrimination, and harassment.

* * *

Our motto for this republic, "All Equal Under Law." That motto stands tall among other nations and unique because we have that motto stamped with the sense of the pursuit of liberty, fraternity, and happiness. Thank god we live in this reshaped American republic of sovereign states. For the glory to have been reshaped for the better, and not for the worst.

II. The Fourteenth Amendment, 1868

Section I, All persons born or naturalized in the United States, and subject to the jurisdiction thereof, are citizens of the United States and of the State wherein they reside. No State shall make or enforce any law which shall abridge the privileges or immunities of citizens of the United States; nor shall any State deprive any person of life, liberty, or property, without due process of law; nor deny to any person within its jurisdiction the equal protection of the laws.

Section II, Representatives shall be apportioned among the several States according to their respective numbers, counting the whole number of persons in each State, excluding Indians not taxed. But when the right to vote at any election for the choice of electors for President and Vice President of the United States, Representatives in Congress, the Executive and Judicial officers of a State, or the members of the Legislature thereof, is denied to any male inhabitants of such State, being twenty-one years of age, and citizens of the United States, or any way abridged, except for participation in rebellion, or other crime, the basis of representation therein shall be reduced in the proportion which the number of such male citizens shall bear to the whole number of male citizens twenty-one years of age in such State.

Section III, No person shall be a Senator or Representative in Congress, or elector of President and Vice President, or hold any office, civil or military, under the United States, or under any State, who having previously taken an oath, as a member of Congress, or as an officer of the United States, or as an executive or judicial officer of any State, to support the Constitution of the United States, shall have engaged in insurrection or rebellion against the same, or given aid or comfort to the enemies thereof. But Congress, may by a vote of two-thirds of each House, remove such disability.

II. The Fourteenth Amendment, 1868

Section IV. The Validity of the public debt of the United States, authorized by law, including debts incurred for payment of pensions and bounties for services in suppressing insurrection or rebellion, shall not be questioned. But neither the United States or any State shall assume or pay any debt or obligation incurred in aid of insurrection or rebellion against the United States, or any claim for the loss or emancipation of any slave, but all such debts, obligations and claims shall be held illegal and void.

Section V. The Congress shall have power to enforce, by appropriate legislation, the provisions of this article.

The racial equality issue has significantly played a critical role in forming our American federalism republic. This country fought a civil war to end slavery. As the national Congress sealed the fate with the passage of the Thirteenth Amendment, and the various sovereign states ratifying it, all people residing and now born in this union are no longer part of the slave caste system. Now comes the question on citizenship for all people residing in this republic.

Now after the civil war and all during to the mid-Twentieth century. White Americans have been violating the rights of the various citizens of different races, color, and creed made into newly persons of this republic. All persons entering this union of sovereign states have a guaranteed civil rights and liberties under the federal constitution. The bill of rights is the American form of protected liberties. But if any state sovereign state government entity fails to protect their citizen's civil liberties, then it is up to the national government entity to step in and enforce these rights and liberties with the appropriate legislation as stated in this chapter's discussion of this new amendment... Amendment number Fourteen.

The Amendments

To add an amendment means a creation of a whole new set of laws open to different views for interpretation. I am not saying the addition of the Fourteenth Amendment to our federal constitution was deemed an error. But it should have been crafted and written better for the understanding of future generations.

The purpose of this amendment, in my constitutional view, was to protect and enforce the already established bill of rights to all persons. The Fourteenth Amendment has an equal protection clause protecting the right of the person for due process, already stated in the Sixth Amendment. I imagine the framers of the Fourteenth wanted to compile all the bill of right amendments into one amendment. Which I see no problem, but it should be applied appropriately regarding each violated case. With enforcement comes funding and I see no problem with that if it is appropriately done and consisted to the violated case. But, unfortunately, since the Fourteenth was laid for the general government to enforce this act…it has taken up to expand on unnecessary funding power and created wasteful spending.

But years after the war was brought to an unconditional surrender of the southern states in rebellion. The newly freed individuals once kept in bondage did not fully obtain full citizenship equality rights filled with our guaranteed liberties.

Many former confederate soldiers and officers that returned to their families and work… began to be making it impossible for these people to flourish as American persons of our society.

In the end, Congress had a job to finish after what they started with the Thirteenth Amendment. That is to promote equality but as well as it guarantees liberty for all persons of all races into this union with a newly made amendment.

II. The Fourteenth Amendment, 1868

I believe that this Constitution had a sharp clean divisionary line between central government and state government powers. The power of immigration and naturalization is declared a rule by Congress. The state governments, respectively the people will decide to enforce it or enforce it on its own. **The federal government can make a rule of declaring all people born and naturalize are citizens of this union, but it is for the states to enforce that rule.**

If the unwise and not needed wisdom of Chief Justice Roger B. Taney could have been spared in defining the naturalization question. We would not have had the clear mess that this union endured and still enduring. But for the Chief Justice, who was a slave owner and quite the racist, I do not hold his opinions to the high regards. But to the minds of a Jefferson, Madison, Gerry, and Sherman would quite be dissenters to his various pretentious opinions.

The national government's high court denied the right of the sovereign states to grant and enforce the naturalization clause in 1842 because of their petty special racist interests. But now a civil war was over and done with, and now this union is trying to reshape into a new union, but with its same federalism principles of liberty and equality. Now the national government, the Congress had evolved into a modern world and began the structure to grant equality and citizenship status to its people.

The authors of the proposed Fourteenth Amendment were two staunch abolitionists that wanted to share the equal rights that they endure onto the other people of different race and color. Senator William P. Fessenden of Maine and Representative Thaddeus Stevens of Pennsylvania.

They wanted to create a union of sovereign states that we all can have the same rights across this nation. If one state cannot guarantee the same rights for one sect of persons, then it can be denied for others. Hence the creation of this powerful and reshaping amendment into our republic.

Section I. All persons born or naturalized in the United States, and subject to the jurisdiction thereof, are citizens of the United States and of the State wherein they reside. No State shall make or enforce any law which shall abridge the privileges or immunities of citizens of the United States; nor shall any State deprive any person of life, liberty, or property, without due process of law; nor deny to any person within its jurisdiction the equal protection of the laws.

As I read Section I of the Fourteenth Amendment, it is quite clear in the language. All people 'born' or 'naturalized' in the United States are citizens of the United States and of the State wherein they reside. Right-wing nationalists are trying to discourage the language of this section of this amendment. They are currently trying to repeal the birthright citizenship status of all persons.

What I do not get regarding this section, is who still the primary enforcer of the naturalization clause? This amendment is just a granted rights to us, the people establishing that we the persons born of natural-born or naturalized are citizens of this union. But I strongly believe the enforcing of this statute still belongs in the hands of each state.

It is not ethical for the national government to take funds from California, New York, and Massachusetts and give those funds to Florida, Illinois, South Carolina for the unconstitutional enforcement of the naturalization clause.

Regarding this amendment, the language remains quite simple to comprehend. The language of the Constitution is

II. The Fourteenth Amendment, 1868

simple to understand but there were and still are individuals that lack constitutional common sense.

Now Section I of the Amendment does not state the race or color or sex of the American person. But it is drastically decreed with all retrospect of common sense that all people born within the realm of these United sovereign States are citizens. Based on the political historical outlook of this nation, we cannot debate that this is what the Framers of this Amendment intended. This amendment was written for all persons, both white, black, of all races to be equal under law.

The Framers of this Amendment grabbed language from Jefferson's Declaration of Independence in adopting it into their language.

"nor shall any State deprive any person of life, liberty, or property, without due process of law;"

All persons can be deprived of life, liberty, or property... but not without due process of the law. We live in a nation of legislations, not of men. We must all abide by them, but not by the person dictating them. All persons are not above the law, this includes from our Chief Executive of this union to the normal person. But we will not be discussing presidential immunity ruling that occurred in 2024. We will be discussing the rule of Congress has to enforce a section among the Fourteenth Amendment.

Let us remember that before the adoption of the Fourteenth Amendment, we have our Ninth Amendment, that guarantees our liberties from any government, both federal and/or state. The issue is not creating more laws to protect the Constitution.

We have seen in the late nineteenth century to current times of people being mistreated with no due process of the law. This is the reason of the adoption of this said

Amendment. And most importantly, that because we had the ignorance of some people not reading the Constitution thoroughly, some problems we incurred back then, are still happening today. Even today, we share the same ignorant individuals that we had back when the Amendment was adopted and supposed to be orchestrated by the appropriate legislation enacted by Congress and properly enforced by the federal executive branch.

We must all put aside all resentment towards a new American union of sovereign States and lift our heads up high as the Americans that we have always been.

"Madam, do not train up your children in hostility to the government of the United States. Remember, we are all one country now. Dismiss from your mind all sectional feeling and bring them up to be Americans." Robert Edward Lee, circa 1870. It was indeed a good quote to be proud to be an American from Robert Edward Lee.

A. Race Relations

One of the terrible rulings affecting the federal government enforcement of the Fourteenth Amendment was not guaranteeing protection to the newly made persons and their right of all their guaranteed freedoms, including the second amendment. And for them to not be able to defend themselves against the threat of a danger to their lives is a disgrace. The right to defend themselves is guaranteed by our Constitution. Or to the extent of federal government protection of their civil liberties and rights is beyond unprecedented. The General Government, at least in this republic is here to protect us from the injustices from public or private dangers, and this government is here to protect us from that danger.

States can find ways to regulate the Second Amendment to protect their residents, but they cannot prohibit or contradict it to anyone. The federal Constitution is a guideline for states and the federal government to obey the rules of federalism and those rules are strictly self-explanatory, to not contradict our principled document.

I am now going to reference different eras of our American republic where state legislators and jurists tended to contradict federal constitutional law on our Second Amendment. From the Black Codes in post-Civil War times to the progressives in the 20th century, there have been constant Second

The Amendments

Amendment contradictions. I am going to discuss the court ruling that finally made it clear to the anti-constitutionalists that nobody, federal officials, state officials, or individuals, have a right to prohibit this right to any person and have no right to contradict the constitution.

Where we see the abuse of a state government contradicting federal constitutional law on the Second Amendment toward its persons, especially the newly made persons of our republic, was in the State of Mississippi. The State of Mississippi's state constitution has a second amendment similar to the federal Constitution's own second amendment.

"Article 1—Declaration of Rights: Sect 23. Every Citizen has a right to bear arms in defence of himself and of the state. (Race and Liberty in America: the essential reader, edited by Jonathan Bean, page 64, Mississippi Constitution, 1832).

To be honest, this right is quite clear. "Every Citizen has a right to bear arms," it says. "Every Citizen." Regardless of social stature, race or background -- every person. And when the Fourteenth Amendment was added to the Constitution, all people born within the realm of this American republic, regardless of skin color, are persons of this nation and of their respective state. There were some members of the white community that were former fighters of the Confederate Army or were descendants of those fighters that had animosity toward these new federal constitutional amendments. These former Confederate individuals still believed that they could return to the Antebellum days of the Old South. The law now prohibited the ownership of slaves, but they still wanted to keep the control over the newly made persons. And how did they gain control, by prohibiting them the free exercise of their Second Amendment rights.

II. The Fourteenth Amendment, 1868

The Magnolia State's legislature passed in 1866 a Black Code to prohibit the new persons from engaging their gun-right privileges.

"Section 1: . . . That no freedman, free negro or mulatto, not in the military service of the United States government, and not licensed so to do by the board of police of his or her county, shall keep or carry fire-arms of any kind, or any ammunition, dirk or bowie knife, and on conviction thereof in the county court shall be punished by fine. . ." (Laws of the State of Mississippi, Passed at a Regular Session of the Mississippi Legislature, December 1865, Race and Liberty in America: the essential reader, edited by Jonathan Bean, page 64, Mississippi Constitution, 1832).

What is the first thing a state cannot do when passing state legislation for their own state? Even though, the Fourteenth Amendment had not been added to the constitution. States were denying basic rights to the newly freed persons from bondage. After the Amendment passed, States cannot contradict the federal constitution. These former slaves became persons of this American republic, and in doing so were guaranteed the same rights and privileges as any other person. Just because the legislators of the Magnolia State fought, or had family members who fought, to preserve a human-rights violation. That did not give them the authority to contradict the federal constitution.

When the federal government realized what these former rebellious states were doing, they enforced federal constitutional law through appropriate legislation allowed in the post-Civil War amendments. This era became known as "Reconstruction." Reconstruction never would have happened if those southern legislators would have accepted defeat and realized they cannot show any form of conflict with the newly reshaped federal Constitution.

The Amendments

Almost a decade after Reconstruction ended, those states had to learn by force not to contradict the constitution. I for one do not like the idea of the federal government using force to impose its will onto a sovereign state, but in the end if states like Mississippi and Louisiana were in violation of a federal Constitutional amendment, then so be it.

Now, in the modern days of our American republic, it is the federal government that is denying persons their Second Amendment privileges. No government, whether federal or state has any right to infringe our rights onto the individual.

The Supreme Court after the Reconstruction years showed its ignorance in trying to interpret the words from the Amendment framers. After the passage of the Amendments were admitted to the federal Constitution, states would be subject to federal government control by a Republican-controlled central government during those times during and after the Civil War.

In 1875, the Supreme Court of the land interpreted that the First Amendment and Second Amendment to the federal Constitution only applied to the federal government and not the states. These were once again ugly times of unnecessary and unproper actions of the federal government.

"We have in our political system a government of the United States and a government of each of the several States. Each of one of these governments is distinct from the others, and each has persons of its own who owe it allegiance, and whose rights, within its jurisdiction, it must protect. The same person may be at the same time a person of the United States and a person of a State, but his rights of citizenship under one of these governments will be different from those he has under the other. *Slaughter-House Cases*, 16 Wall. 74."

(Opinion Brief of U.S v. Cruikshank, 92 U.S. 542, (1875), Chief Justice Morrison Waite).

II. The Fourteenth Amendment, 1868

You cannot be a sword with two blades. The Fourteenth Amendment framers authored this article for all of us to be persons of these United States of America. The Constitution does not give privilege to one sect of individuals and deny it to others.

Yes, every colony ... state is different from one another. Every state will have the ability to have its own sovereignty and autonomy to make its own set of laws that govern its residents. The federal Constitution must remain the guiding principle in creating their own state laws. These articles were an added enforcement power of the national government, whether we the states...respectively the people were upset with these newly added amendments. They are within the national constitution and must be respected and maintained. But what led to various states denying the basic rights to their different residents of therein state. Is that there was quite rebellious Supreme Court that decided to evade the true and now revised meaning of the constitution. The constitution can be revised...hence to reshape this republic for the better good for this union.

I have always said that the civil war amendments reshaped this union for the greater glory and liberty as prescribed in it and in our declaration of independence. Other amendments, two of them added to the constitution were not needed and added additional unprincipled powers.

"The government of the United States is one of delegated powers alone. Its authority is defined and limited by the Constitution. All powers not granted to it by that instrument are reserved to the States or the people. No rights can be acquired under the constitution or laws of the United States, except such as the government of the United States has the authority to grant and secure. All that cannot be granted or secured are left under the protection of the States." (Opinion Brief of U.S v. Cruikshank, 92 U.S. 542, (1875), Chief Justice Morrison Waite).

The Amendments

"We now proceed to an examination of the indictment, to ascertain whether the several rights, which it is alleged the defendants intended to interfere with, are such as had been law in fact granted or secured by the constitution or laws of the United States" (Opinion Brief of U.S v. Cruikshank, 92 U.S. 542, (1875), Chief Justice Morrison Waite).

This whole case happened because of an electoral dispute after the 1872 elections in Louisiana. A federal judge ruled that the Republican-majority legislature can be seated. There was widespread resentment of this ruling by many members of the Democratic Party and former confederate rebels. And so, many of those members took to the streets and attacked newly freed black persons and other persons. Under the federal legislation of the Enforcement Act of 1870, those Democrat agitators were charged, and the victims of this attack protested that the attackers violated their First, Second, Fourteenth, and Fifteenth Amendment rights. This is truly the first case where we saw that various states, in the south, and the federal government were contradicting the newly added amendments, but also our bill of rights.

"The first and ninth counts state the intent of the defendants to have been to hinder and prevent the persons named in the free exercise and enjoyment of their 'lawful right and privilege to peaceably to assemble together with each other and with other persons of the United States for a peaceful and lawful purpose.' The right of the people peaceably to assemble for lawful purposes existed long before the adoption of the Constitution of the United States. In fact, it is, and always has been, one of the attributes of citizenship under a free government. It 'derives its source,' to use the language of Chief Justice Marshall, in *Gibbons v. Ogden*, 9 Wheat. 211, 'from those laws whose authority is acknowledged by civilized man throughout the world.' It is found wherever

II. The Fourteenth Amendment, 1868

civilization exists. It was not, therefore, a right granted to the people by the constitution. The government of the United States when established found it in existence, with the obligation on the part of the States to afford it protection. As no direct power over it was granted to Congress it remains according to the ruling in *Gibbons v. Ogden*, id. 203, subject to state jurisdiction. *552 Only such existing rights were committed by the people to the protection of Congress as came within the general scope of the authority granted to the national government." (Opinion Brief of U.S v. Cruikshank, 92 U.S. 542, (1875), Chief Justice Morrison Waite).

Supreme Court rulings are supposed to reflect the law or dissident in question. It was never meant for the court to whip out their own special interests above any strict constitutional interests. This new high court of the land were promoting the agenda of white supremacy over the newly freed persons of minority decent. They were denying the newly made persons their right to bear arms as instructed in our second amendment and other bill of right amendments.

In *Gibbon v. Ogden*, Marshall and the court were discussing the very idea of the Commerce Clause and navigational trade among across the several sovereign states and if there would be any interference from the central government. What does the Commerce Clause have to do with the Colfax Massacre? Absolutely, nothing, it was just political theater to give credibility to the agitators and a reason to protest and protect their application of their "supposed" innocence.

The First Amendment is a 'Catch-22' argument from our founders. It is called being tolerant and non-violent. The words in this Amendment say it all: "Or the right of the people peaceably to assemble...." It does not advocate inciting violence from either side. There will be individuals or groups of individuals you may not agree with, but it is

The Amendments

your right to listen or ignore, just as it is their right to say their grievances without a show of force. This was pure constitutional wisdom from our constitutional framers.

"'The scope and application of these amendments are no longer subjects of discussion here.' They left the authority of the States just where they found it and added nothing to the already existing powers of the United States." (Opinion Brief of U.S v. Cruikshank, 92 U.S. 542, (1875), Chief Justice Morrison Waite).

The federal constitution gives each individual state the right to enforce the amendments to our Constitution, but to make sure that no laws are contradictory to them. If states decide to not enforce a valid federal constitutional amendment and began to show privilege to one race and not the other race. Then it is the duty of the federal government's national Congress to administer and advise the states in rebellion the appropriate steps to follow the constitution with appropriate federal legislation. Hence, the unfortunate era of Reconstruction.

"The second and tenth counts are equally defective. The right there specified is that of 'bearing arms for a lawful purpose.' This is not a right granted by the Constitution. Neither is it any manner dependent upon that instrument for its existence. The second amendment declares that it shall not be infringed; but this, as has been seen, means no more than that it shall not be infringed by Congress. This is one of the amendments that has no other effect than to restrict the powers of the national government, leaving the people to look for their protection against any violation by their fellow-persons of the rights it recognizes, to what is called, in The City of New York v. Miln, 11 Pet. 139, the 'powers which relate to merely municipal legislation, or what was, perhaps, more properly called internal police', 'not surrendered or

II. The Fourteenth Amendment, 1868

restrained' by the Constitution of the United States." (Opinion Brief of U.S v. Cruikshank, 92 U.S. 542, (1875), Chief Justice Morrison Waite).

If a person, or group of persons, regardless of race, attacks another, the persons being attacked have every right to defend themselves and use their right of the Second Amendment for that protection. To blatantly suggest that only a group of people have that right but not others, is giving privilege to the law to one group of persons but not the other. That is not in the constitution. It clearly states, "All persons born within the realm of the United States and territories are persons."

The following is the chief justice's explanation for giving privileges to one race of persons but not the other:

"The Fourteenth Amendment prohibits a State from depriving any person of life, liberty or property, without due process of law; but this adds nothing to the rights of one person as against another. It simply furnishes an additional guaranty against any encroachment by the States upon the fundamental rights which belong to every person as a member of society. As was paid by Mr. Justice Johnson, in Bank of Columbia v. Okely, 4 Wheat. 244, it secures 'the individual from the arbitrary exercise of the powers of government, unrestrained by the established principles of private and distributive justice.' These principles in the indictment do not call for the exercise of any of the powers conferred by this provision in the amendment." (Opinion Brief of U.S v. Cruikshank, 92 U.S. 542, (1875), Chief Justice Morrison Waite).

"The fourth and twelve counts charge the intent to have been to prevent and hinder the persons named, who were of African descent and persons of color, in 'the free exercise and enjoyment of their several right and privilege to the full and equal benefit of all laws and proceedings, then and there, before that time, enacted or ordained by the said State of Louisiana and by the United States; and then and there, at that time, being in force in the State and District of Louisiana aforesaid, for the security of their respective persons and property, then and there, at that time enjoyed at and within said the State and District of Louisiana by white persons, being persons of said State of Louisiana and the United States, for the protection of the persons and property of said white persons.' There is no allegation that this was done because of the race or color of the persons conspired against. When stripped of its verbiage, the case as presented amounts to nothing more than that the defendants conspired to prevent certain persons of the United States, being within the State of Louisiana, from enjoying the equal protection of the laws of the State and of the United States." (Opinion Brief of U.S v. Cruikshank, 92 U.S. 542, (1875), Chief Justice Morrison Waite).

There you have it, folks, the first jurist trying to override a lawful federal constitutional amendment and rewrite the amendment himself. The civil war amendments were written after the bloody conflict that was fought to end the human-rights violations of slavery and discrimination. These amendments, including the Fourteenth Amendment, consist of equal protection and due process of the law for all persons regardless of race. We already have a bill of rights amendments, the Fourteenth just reassures that right.

Unfortunately, because we have had ill-sensed individuals and quite ignorant to the rules of federalism...therefore we have the federal government we have today. If these former confederate, white individuals would have just gone home to their shops and farms after the civil war and understood the reshaping structure of this republic. Then the federal government would not have increased their powers, not only on civil rights but on naturalization, infrastructure, and social programs.

II. The Fourteenth Amendment, 1868

"No question arises under the Civil Rights Act of April 9, 1866 (14 Stat. 27), which is intended for the protection of persons of the United States in the enjoyment of certain rights, without discrimination on account of race, color, or previous condition of servitude, because as has already been stated, it is nowhere alleged in these counts that the wrong contemplated against the rights of these persons was on account of their race or color." (Opinion Brief of U.S v. Cruikshank, 92 U.S. 542, (1875), Chief Justice Morrison Waite).

Many of these agitators who attacked this peaceful assembly of black persons were white. This ruling was and only to contemplate satisfaction of white privilege which at the time was the majority race in America. The constitution with the Fourteenth Amendment sees no color, only sees equality.

"I concur that the judgment in this case should be arrested, but for the reasons quite different from those given by the court." (Dissenting Brief of U.S v. Cruikshank, 92 U.S. 542, (1875), Associate Justice Nathan Clifford).

"Persons born on naturalized in the United States, and subject to the jurisdiction thereof, are persons thereof; and the fourteenth amendment also provides, that no State shall make or enforce any law which shall abridge the privileges or immunities of persons of the United States. Congress may, doubtless, prohibit any violation of that provision, and may provide that any person convicted of violating the same shall be guilty of an offence, and be subject to such reasonable punishment as Congress may prescribe." (Dissenting Brief of U.S v. Cruikshank, 92 U.S. 542, (1875), Associate Justice Nathan Clifford).

"What is charged in the fourteenth count is, that the defendants did combine, conspire, and confederate the said persons of African descent and persons of color to injure, oppress, threaten, and intimidate, with the intent the said persons thereby to prevent and hinder in the free exercise and enjoyment of the right and privilege to vote *at any election to be thereafter had and held* according to law by the people of the State, or by the people of the parish; they, the defendants, well knowing that the said persons were lawfully qualified to vote at any such election thereafter to be had and held." (Dissenting Brief of U.S v. Cruikshank, 92 U.S. 542, (1875), Associate Justice Nathan Clifford).

Justice Nathan Clifford is quite clear in how our rules of federalism must be applied in our American federalism republic. The federal constitution is the principled governing document that governs our individual and sovereign rights, and we must abide to it.

And another valid and constitutional point, Justice Clifford points out is that the said victims of the altercation were within their legal and rightful bounds to participate in the American electoral process without the hint of oppression, threat, or cause of injury or death.

The First Amendment was put in place to be accepting of all forms of speech and opinion without the use of agitation or force. There will be views of other persons that we may not like or agree with, but it is our duty as persons to simply ignore it. And if our rights are threatened by a voice of opposition then it is our right as persons of this country to invoke the Second Amendment. These two amendments are equally important to preserve, protect and maintain our republic.

"Certain other causes for arresting the judgment are assigned in the record, which deny the constitutionality of the Enforcement Act; but, having come to the conclusion that the indictment is insufficient, it is not necessary to consider that question." (Dissenting Brief of U.S v. Cruikshank, 92 U.S. 542, (1875), Associate Justice Nathan Clifford).

II. The Fourteenth Amendment, 1868

The Enforcement Act of 1870 was a congressional enforcement tool to enforce the Fifteenth Amendment, not the Fourteenth Amendment. These newly made persons were within their constitutional right to exercise their right to free speech, as well as their right to vote. And if their right to free speech was abridged, then they are within their right use their second amendment. The Fourteenth Amendment is a safeguard safety net tool to enforce the bill of rights, especially the due process amendment.

To recognize the newly made persons of this republic, and to guarantee their basic constitutional right protections. I believe the national Congress has in its power to enact legislation to protect all their bill of rights. But sadly, politicians like to create amendments and pass laws after laws without first considering the first initiative. The Constitution is there for the protection of all citizens and within added the Fourteenth Amendment. It is now consisted that all persons are within citizens, not withstanding their race, color, or sex.

Unfortunately, in those times after the civil war and in segregation times, neither the federal government nor several state governments enforced the constitutional rights as listed in the bill of rights of the Fourteenth. And here comes my response to my first question. Yes, it was necessary for the national Congress to establish the Fourteenth Amendment. This amendment made it quite clear in its language that the national Congress will have its authority to grant legislative enforcement to the federal executive branch. Federal enforcement legislative action to truly guarantee all persons the right to equality under law and its due process guarantee.

And so, I agree with Justice Nathan Clifford in his dissenting opinion. Federal and state governments cannot let dogs lie and ignore the federal constitution. It truly goes against our rules of federalism. Once the state breaks these rules, you will have anarchy and further infiltration of the federal government, which is one thing our Founding Fathers never dreamed would happen. And so, I dissent to these civil rights and slaughter-house cases against our constitution and equality under law clauses.

* * *

One Supreme Court ruling presented itself to set our country back in the progress of liberty and equality. In 1896, the Supreme Court ruled that a Louisiana state law was constitutional, and it created the beginning of segregation. With a double standard law precedent of "separate but equal" clause on the Federal Constitution. As we all know that Louisiana state law and other state laws that passed segregation laws were indeed unconstitutional in PRINCIPLE. They were in constant contradiction to our newly reshaped republic's meaning.

The story behind the 1896 case of *Plessy v. Ferguson*, is indeed quite contradictory to the federal constitution and to any constitutional thinking American. On the 7th of June 1892, a black American person purchased a first-class ticket on the East Louisiana Railway, from New Orleans to Covington, two destinations within the same state of Louisiana. He was then forcibly asked to relinquish that first-class seat in which he paid for and to move back to a third-class seat. He denied and so he was aggressively removed from the train and immediately sent off to jail. The man was charged with violating an act passed by the Louisiana General Assembly on July 10, 1890. This state case was indeed appealed to the highest court of the land and the highest court did hear it and gave an unfortunate ruling against this American person, who happened to be black.

II. The Fourteenth Amendment, 1868

"This case turns up upon the constitutionality of an act of the general assembly of the state of Louisiana, passed in 1890, providing for separate railway carriages for the whites and colored races. Acts 1890, No. 111, p. 152." (Opinion Brief of Plessy v. Ferguson, Associate Justice Henry Billings Brown).

"The first section of the statute enacts "that all railway companies carrying passengers in their coaches in this state, shall provide equal but separate accommodations for the white, and colored races, by providing two or more passenger coaches by a partition so as to secure separate accommodations: provided, that this section shall not be construed to apply to street railroads. No person or persons shall be permitted to occupy these seats in coaches, other than the ones assigned to them, on account of the race they belong to." (Opinion Brief of Plessy v. Ferguson, Associate Justice Henry Billings Brown).

Justice Henry B. Brown concocted a dream-world analogy that this case was constitutional. The state law states that all coaches must have equal but separate accommodations but in the real world, that was not the case. If the coaches were supposed to have separate accommodations for people based on race, then why did not have a first-class coach for both white and black races? If the 'separate but equal' proponents wanted to continue to defend this outcome. Then truly they should have created a first-class coach for whites and one for blacks, the same for second- and third-class coach cars. This Louisiana state law and later state education laws contradicted the national Constitution.

Homer Plessy bought a first-class ticket because it is his right as a legal American person. It is not the fault of this individual that a bunch of contradicting and discriminative state legislators from the Pelican State cannot write a legislation without being sane with common sense. That is the problem with legislators of today, that they write legislations with emotions and not with their minds. The only people that get hurt are the American individual.

"...any passenger insisting on going into a coach or compartment to which by race he does not belong to, shall be liable to a fine of twenty-five dollars, or in lieu thereof to imprisonment for a period of not more than twenty days in the parish prison..." (Opinion Brief of Plessy v. Ferguson, Associate Justice Henry Billings Brown).

This law is not only a violation of the Fourteenth Amendment that clearly violates the "equal" protection clause of the law, but it sure violates the Eighth Amendment. I believe this amendment was quite underrated and forgotten that many public officials have ignored it to pass ridiculous and bigoted, if not racist laws and ordinances. Back in those days, the amount of twenty-five dollars would be the equivalent of one-hundred dollars, it was a lot of money. And to imprison an American person for simply exercising his constitutional right as guaranteed in the constitution just because some states decided to be contradictive is wrong.

The framers of this amendment wanted their American citizenry, when committed of a harsh crime and found guilty of that crime. That the punishment fit the harsh crime. But for an individual to suffer a punishment for trying to obtain a first-class ticket seat, that is a clear violation of the Eighth Amendment.

Now Justice Henry Brown targets that this state law does not conflict with the thirteenth and fourteenth amendments. It most definitely does conflict with these civil war amendments. It is no different than a state denying the right of an American person the right to carry and bear arms as guaranteed in the second amendment.

"The constitutionality of this act is attacked upon the ground that it conflicts both with the thirteenth amendment

II. The Fourteenth Amendment, 1868

of the constitution, abolishing slavery, and the fourteenth amendment, which prohibits certain restrictive legislation on the part of the states." (Opinion Brief of Plessy v. Ferguson, Associate Justice Henry Billings Brown).

"1. That it does not conflict with the thirteenth amendment, which abolished slavery and involuntary servitude, except as a punishment for crime, is too clear for argument. Slavery implies involuntary servitude—a state of bondage; the ownership of mankind as a chattel, or, at least, the control of the labor and services of one man for the benefit of another, and the absence of a legal right to the disposal of his own person, property, and services." (Opinion Brief of Plessy v. Ferguson, Associate Justice Henry Billings Brown).

Whereas this law is not forcing in the separation of coaches, the idea of slavery of involuntary servitude by race. They are creating the same separation principles and ideas during the antebellum days of the south. These legislators that passed this act were grandchildren of former Confederate soldiers and public officials during the civil war. And they feel a certain resentment of the central government passing three federal constitutional amendments that gave persons of a colored race, the right to be Americans. So, they would do anything in their power to think with their emotions and not their minds and contradict federal constitutional law to benefit their agenda. So, the idea of forcing people to work for free and in bondage was no longer an issue but the idea of keeping the races separate as they were in an antebellum plantation was alive and well and it was blatant unconstitutional.

To see Justice Brown twist and turn and make look that this law is constitutional and not in conflict with the civil war amendments is insulting to every constitutional scholar that has studied the constitution, its laws and rulings applied

The Amendments

to its revered reshaped document. Now comes another where the unconstitutional jurists have twisted and turned the verbiage of this amendment into their own language for personal reasons and agenda, the Fourteenth Amendment. This amendment is clear in its language, that all persons born or naturalized in this country shall receive equal treatment under law to all its persons by race.

"The proper construction of this amendment was first called to the attention of this court in the Slaughter-House Cases, 16 Wall. 36, which involved, however, not a question of race, but one of exclusive privileges. The case did not call any expression of opinion as to the exact rights it was intended to secure to the colored race, but it was said generally that its main purpose was to establish the persons of the negro, to give definitions of persons of the United States and of the states, and to protect from the hostile legislation of the states the privileges and immunities of persons of the United States, as distinguished from those of persons of the states." (Opinion Brief of Plessy v. Ferguson, Associate Justice Henry Billings Brown).

To create separate schools, restaurants, transportation accommodations, water fountains based on race is blatantly unconstitutional. It is a clear violation of our constitutional sense of initial liberty and then a sense of reshaping equality.

As I have said before and will continue in saying it in various several chapters of this book. Is that states can pass any legislation, they see fit, for the majority of their voting residents. Just as these laws are not in contradiction to the constitution. When I say states, all states, from Maine to Florida, to Virginia to California. All states must abide to the laws in the constitution to create a more perfect union and the central government is an administrative power, in various cases, in making sure the union remains at peace.

II. The Fourteenth Amendment, 1868

Justice Brown then brings examples of other states that have placed segregation policies to separate the colored races among the white races. He fails to grasp the reality of the constitutional situation, no state whether southern or northern can discriminate and to allow an equal opportunity to all and equality under law.

"One of the earliest of these cases is that of *Roberts v. City of Boston*, 5 Cush. 198, in **1141 which the supreme judicial court of Massachusetts held that the general school committee of Boston had power to make provision for the instruction of colored children in separate schools established exclusively for them, and to prohibit their attendance upon the other schools." (Opinion Brief of Plessy v. Ferguson, Associate Justice Henry Billings Brown).

This court ruling in the New England state of Massachusetts occurred in 1850, the height of racial inequality and slavery was still a debated human rights issue down south. What Justice Brown failed to neglect to tell in his opinion brief has significant cause for the idea of liberty. In 1855, the defendant that was once denied entry to a school and with the help of then-senator Charles Sumner passed in the General Assembly of that state, a ban on segregated schools within the Commonwealth of Massachusetts. This was acted before the Fourteenth Amendment was enacted into our constitution. Massachusetts was the first to recognize that all races in her state and then in the entire country is that all races are equal under law.

If people would have revolted against Justice Brown's ridiculous opening brief. This ruling would have never taken place. He brings another example of a state that enacted separate but equal accommodations but will be shot down by my analogy and made into a laughingstock of a jurist.

The Amendments

"Laws forbidding the intermarriage of the two races may be said in a technical sense to interfere with the freedom of contract, and yet have been universally recognized as within the police power of the state. State v. Gibson, 36 Ind. 389." (Opinion Brief of Plessy v. Ferguson, Associate Justice Henry Billings Brown).

Why would be the business of the state let alone the central government when two people want to share their life together and they just happened to be of different races. Not only its nobody's business and secondly it goes truly goes against the Fourteenth Amendment regardless to what the Supreme Court of Indiana stated or Justice Henry Billings Brown. It took this country, one-hundred years later to finally recognize the idea of interracial marriage that is a constitutional law, and that central, state, and local law enforcement has no right to impose any segregated policy against a married or non-common law couple, 1967 supreme court ruling of *Loving v. Virginia.*

"The distinction between laws interfering with the political equality of the negro and those requiring the separation of the two races in schools, theaters, and railway carriages has been frequently drawn by this court. Thus, in *Strauder v. West Virginia*, 100 U.S. 303, it was held that a law of West Virginia limiting to white male persons 21 years of age, and persons of the state, the right to sit upon juries, was a discrimination which implied a legal inferiority in civil society, which lessened the security of the right of the colored race and was a step towards reducing them to a condition of servility. Indeed, the right of a colored man that, in selection of jurors to pass upon his life, liberty, and property, shall be no exclusion of his race, and no discrimination against them because of color, has been asserted in number of cases." (Opinion Brief of Plessy v. Ferguson, Associate Justice Henry Billings Brown).

II. The Fourteenth Amendment, 1868

The state of West Virginia was wrong in establishing this law to create divisions among the jury system based on the color of the person's skin. Every person of this country deserves equal treatment under the law especially when it comes when a black American is on trial. This law was extremely unconstitutional and contradicting to federal constitutional law that the Supreme Court ruled against it.

Justice Brown fought to persuade the court and the nation that they were no similarities towards these two state laws. There are similarities within each state laws, but a clear distinction within the constitution. These state laws and the constitution share a contradictory opinion and should have been stricken down by the high court. Justice John Marshall Harlan gave his dissenting opinion to this ruling and he had something to say on the court's *Plessy's* opinion regarding, *Strauder v. West Virginia.*

"It was consequently, adjudged that a state law that excluded persons of the colored race from juries, because of their race, however well qualified in other respects to discharge the duties of jurymen, was repugnant to the fourteenth amendment. At the present term, referring to the previous adjudications, this court declared that "underlying all of those decisions is the principle that the constitution of the United States, in its present form, forbids, so far as civil and political rights are concerned, discrimination by the general government or the states against any person because of his race." (Dissenting Brief of Plessy v. Ferguson, Associate Justice John Marshall Harlan).

"All citizens are equal before the law."
Associate Justice John Marshall Harlan

"All persons are equal before the law." It is quite stated that we call on for everyone living in this union of sovereign states that we are all people to be treated with the same liberty, rights, and justice under the law. The Constitution now calls for it, and we must continue to share that same calling.

"Finally, and to the end of that no person should be denied, on account of his race, the privilege of participating in the political control of his country, it was declared by the fifteenth amendment that 'the right of persons of the United States to vote shall not be denied or abridged by the United States or by any state on account of race, color or previous condition of servitude.'" (Dissenting Brief of Plessy v. Ferguson, Associate Justice John Marshall Harlan).

Justice Harlan made it abundantly clear that the voting rights and political participation of all persons should not be infringed regardless of race or color. But many states in the south and west disregarded his dissenting brief with extreme prejudice and continue to contradict the federal constitution until 1967.

Many people had different opinions of Associate Justice John Marshall Harlan. But one thing for sure is that he was a constitutional, equal common-sense jurist...well, sometimes. (On the opinions and issues of taxation, he was laying the framework to a massive federal government bureaucracy of extreme direct taxation and spending.) Former Associate Justice Thurgood Marshall during his fights for racial equality based his briefs on many John M. Harlan's quotes.

An aide to NAACP lawyer Thurgood Marshall recalled: "Marshall had a 'Bible' to which he turned during his most depressed moments...Marshall would read aloud passages from Harlan's amazing dissent. I do not believe we ever filed a major brief in the pre-Brown days in which a portion of that opinion was quoted. Marshall's favorite quote was, 'Our constitution is color-blind. It became our basic creed.'" (Race

II. The Fourteenth Amendment, 1868

& Liberty in America, The Essential Reader, Edited by Jonathan Bean, The Independent Institute, 2009, page 111).

Whether if the state is in the south, north, east, or west, it must abide by the constitution in its current reshaped form and apply it to modern times. If the fourteenth amendment in the constitution states that "all persons are equal under the law" and "equal treatment under law", then these two statements must not be refuted and must be obeyed. Sadly, in most southern states, there was still some resentment from descendants of confederate soldiers that felt to keep the races separate and having total disregard for our principled document.

Regardless of the outcome of the civil war, and the laws that were passed after that episode in United States history, people must abide to the constitution and leave their personal feelings, anger, and bitterness behind and focus on moving the country in a more positive sense.

"In delivering the opinion of the court (Civil Rights Cases, 109 U.S. 3, 3 Sup. Ct. 18), Mr. Justice Bradley observed that the fourteenth amendment 'does not invest congress with power to legislate upon subjects that are within the *547 domain of state legislation, but to provide modes of relief against **1142 state legislation or state action of the kind referred to. It does not authorize congress to create a code of municipal law for the regulation of private rights, but to provide modes of redress against the operation of state laws, and the action of state officers, executive or judicial, when these are subversive of the fundamental rights specified in the amendment." (Opinion Brief of Plessy v. Ferguson, Associate Justice Henry Billings Brown).

Justices Bradley and Brown are wrong when they stated that "The Fourteenth Amendment does not invest congress with power to legislate upon the subjects that are within the domain of state legislation". The Amendment's fifth section clearly states that "The Congress shall have power to enforce, by appropriate legislation, the provisions of this article".

"Positive rights and privileges are undoubtedly secured by the fourteenth amendment; but they are secured by way of prohibition against state laws and state proceedings affecting those rights and privileges, and by power given to congress to legislate for the purpose of carrying such prohibition into effect; and such legislation must be necessarily be predicated upon such supposed state laws or state proceedings and be directed to the correction of their operation and effect." (Opinion Brief of Plessy v. Ferguson, Associate Justice Henry Billings Brown).

"You cannot have your cake and eat it too." Justices Bradley and Brown cannot pick and choose how the federal constitutional law of the fourteenth amendment must be enforced and applied. The amendment is quite clear. Congress has the power to ensure to enforce the amendment by form of legislation to ensure that all states must comply.

"While we think the enforced separation of the races, as applied to the internal commerce of the state, neither abridges the privileges or immunities of the colored man, deprives him of his property without due process of law, nor denies him the equal protection of the laws, within the meaning of the fourteenth amendment, we are not prepared to say that the conductor, in assigning passengers to the coaches according to their race, does not act at his peril, or that the provision of the second section of the act that denies to the passenger compensation *549 in damages for a refusal to receive him into the coach in which he properly belongs is a valid exercise of the legislative power." (Opinion Brief of Plessy v. Ferguson, Associate Justice Henry Billings Brown).

II. The Fourteenth Amendment, 1868

But one thing that Justice Brown must realize is that the Louisiana state law is refusing to offer the same privileges and immunities to a colored person as he is offering to a white person. The issue is not "separation of races", but a "separation of class" in which the white race belongs in a first-class coach car and the colored race belongs in second-class or third-class coach car. As Justice Harlan put it in his dissent that America does not and has never been established to have a caste system. Even during the antebellum era, America's founding principled documents never spoke of a caste system. Regardless of obscured statements from people like Roger Taney, or James Mason.

The state law clearly states, "that all railway companies carrying passengers in their coaches in this state, shall provide equal but separate accommodations for the white, and colored races". The first-class section is a coach in which is a passenger coach, why isn't the first-class passenger coach divided into separate partitions? The legislators of the Louisiana General Assembly are not only post-confederate sympathizers but act as if they were part of the antebellum upper-class society.

The state law is denying the colored races, their privileges, and immunities as American persons and therefore a strict contradiction to federal constitutional law which applies to all states.

Now there was a sole dissenting voice in this court hearing, but Justice John Marshall Harlan's dissent speaks a thousand words and more constitutional than the opinion brief.

"In respect of civil rights, common to all persons, the constitution of the United States does not, I think permit any public authority to know the race of those entitled to be protected in the enjoyment of such rights. Every true man has pride of race, and under appropriate circumstances, when the rights of others, his equals before the law, are not to be affected, it is his privilege to express such pride and to take such action based upon it as to him seems proper. But I deny that any legislative body or judicial tribunal may have regard to the ***555** race of persons when the civil rights of those persons are involved. Indeed, such legislation as that here in question is inconsistent not only with that equality of rights which pertains to personship, national and state, but with the personal liberty enjoyed by everyone within the United States." (Dissenting Brief of Plessy v. Ferguson, Associate Justice John Marshall Harlan).

Justice Harlan made it quite clear in his dissenting opinion, that the rights of every American regardless of race should not be infringed by any power of the central or state governments. The United States of America has always respected its persons and now we must respect our respected person on the account of race whether these states like it or not.

"I am of opinion that the state of Louisiana is inconsistent with the personal liberty of persons, white and black, in that state, and hostile to both the spirit and letter of the constitution of the United States. If laws of like character should be enacted in the several states of the Union, the effect would be in the highest degree mischievous. Slavery, as an institution tolerated by law, would, it is true, have disappeared from our country; but there would remain a power in the states, by sinister legislation, to interfere with the full enjoyment of freedom, to regulate civil rights, common to all persons, upon the basis of race, and to place in a condition of legal inferiority a large body of American persons, now constituting a part of the political community, called the ***564** 'People of the United States,' for whom, and by whom through representatives, our government is administered. Such a system is inconsistent with the guaranty given by the constitution to

II. The Fourteenth Amendment, 1868

each state of a republican form of government, and may be stricken down by congressional action, or by the courts in the discharge of their solemn duty to maintain the supreme law of the land, anything in the constitution or laws of any state to the contrary notwithstanding. For the reason stated, I am constrained to withhold my assent from the opinion and judgment of the majority." (Dissenting Brief of Plessy v. Ferguson, Associate Justice John Marshall Harlan).

Besides the word, inconsistent, I would also have included in describing Louisiana's legislative statute, "contradictory" to the federal constitution. As I have said earlier, the idea of slavery perished from the existence of our American republic way of life but there remains the horrible stench of a sour mint julep of racism in the former rebellious states and newly western states. And the descendants of the confederate rebels wanted to show their ancestors that they were once again bringing the old days of the antebellum society. Slavery was indeed gone but the idea of separating the races was not and they were going to pursue it no matter how far they will go in breaking federal constitutional law. But what these legislators of the Pelican state did and other legislators across the south and other parts of the country did was not only inconsistent or contradictory to our constitution. And for that, I join in with Associate Justice John M. Harlan and dissent against this opinion and ruling.

"[Such] a construction [of the Privileges or Immunities Clause] followed by the reversal of the judgments of the Supreme Court of Louisiana in these cases, would constitute this court q perpetual censor upon all legislation of the States, on the civil rights of their own persons, with authority to nullify such as it did not approve as consistent with those rights, as they existed at the time of the adoption of this amendment." (Opinion of the Court of the Slaughter-House Cases, 83 U.S. at 78, Associate Justice Samuel Freeman, 1873).

"We are convinced that no such results were intended by the Congress which proposed these amendments, nor by the legislatures of the States which ratified them." (Opinion of the Court of the Slaughter-House Cases, 83 U.S. at 78, Associate Justice Samuel Freeman, 1873).

Especially after the several sovereign states ratified Amendment Fourteen.

The Court is not here to be convinced by the Constitution. The Court is here to interpret the Constitution correctly and to reshape the republic accordingly. The Amendment's language is quite clear for what entity or entities are supposed to enforce and follow. If the Congress that proposed and passed this amendment and later the state legislatures ratified the said amendment were as slow as the future generations to understand this piece of act…then this union will be doomed with blatant ignorance.

"It is objected that the power conferred is novel and large. The answer is that the novelty was known, and the measure deliberately adopted… It is necessary to enable the government of the nation to secure to everyone within its jurisdiction the rights and privileges enumerated, which, according to the plainest considerations of reason and justice and the fundamental principles of the social compact, all are entitled to enjoy. Without such authority, any government claiming to be national is glaringly defective." (Dissenting Opinion of the Court of the Slaughter-House Cases, 83 U.S. at 78, Associate Justice Noah H. Swayne, 1873).

After one of the bloodiest civil wars this union endured. We received new enumerated powers for the national government and a mutual respect from federal and state governments on these new powers. They are powers granted for the protection of all persons' equal liberty and rights as persons.

II. The Fourteenth Amendment, 1868

If the high court did not endure to restrict the sovereign states to offer freedom and individual liberty. Then we would not have endured a civil war conflict. But the matter of fact, we did endure in a bloody, unfortunate civil war conflict and the national Congress passed new powers onto them. So, we must understand this amendment and respect them

The authority was legally granted by our national legislature, and then ratified by most of the state legislatures to be added to their Constitution. Despite what people mostly from the south ignorantly claim that this amendment was passed with illegality and coercion...there is no factual evidence to that effect.

* * *

After the unconstitutional ruling of *Plessy v. Ferguson* was upheld and the statute of "Separate but Equal" began to create disharmony across our union. This disharmony plagued our struggling republic for many years. Even though there have been cases *Plessy* that have claimed that this statute was contradictory to the federal constitution. America would not see the final eyes of equality justice until 1967. But sometimes, the public remains ignorant, close-minded, and unaware on what the supreme court has dictated.

In 1917, there was a supreme court ruling that made the *Plessy* decision to be unconstitutional and overturned. All those "separate but equal" state legislations across this union should have been null and void. It is a shame that it took almost fifty years for the United States of America to finally embrace liberty and equality. But all could have been avoided, all the civil rights brawls and fights if the people and public officials of each autonomous states would have respected the constitution. The ruling that should have sealed the fate of

The Amendments

Plessy v. Ferguson and the end of racial segregation came to play in 1917, with the court ruling of *Buchanan v. Warley*. "In the court of original jurisdiction in Kentucky, and in the Court of Appeals of that state, the case was made to turn upon the constitutional validity of the ordinance. The Court of Appeals of Kentucky, 165 Ky. 559, 177 S. W. 472, Ann. Cas. 1917B, 149, held the ordinance valid and of itself a complete defense to the action." "The title of the ordinance is: 'An ordinance to prevent conflict and ill-feeling between the white and colored races in the City of Louisville, and to preserve the public peace and promote the general welfare, by making reasonable provisions requiring, as far as practicable, the use of separate blocks, for residences, places of abode, and places of assembly by white and colored people respectively.'" (Opinion Brief of Buchanan v. Warley, Associate Justice William R. Day).

In reading this ordinance what the City of Louisville, Kentucky lay upon its person residents was despicable and unconstitutional. The state of Kentucky never joined the Confederate States of America, but they did share one common interest, their economic source of slavery. And so, when the Thirteenth Amendment and Fourteenth Amendment entered our constitution. Many Kentuckians felt resentment towards the general government. And so, like the state of Louisiana and other states alike, passed similar laws and ordinances to create a buffer zone and used the term "separate but equal" to maintain the old antebellum days of the old south.

This Kentucky ordinance reached the supreme court of the land to truly interpret if it should stand as is or shot it down for one reason, that it was unconstitutional to our federal constitution.

II. The Fourteenth Amendment, 1868

"The assignments of error in this court attack the ordinance upon the ground that it violated the Fourteenth Amendment of the Constitution of the United States, in that it abridges the privileges and immunities of persons of the United States to acquire and enjoy property, takes property without due process of the law, and denies equal protection of the laws." "This court has frequently held that while an unconstitutional act is no law, attacks upon the validity of laws can only be entertained when made by those whose rights are directly affected by the law or ordinance in question." (Opinion Brief of Buchanan v. Warley, Associate Justice William R. Day).

This ordinance clearly violates the Fourteenth Amendment. As the state law of Louisiana violated this amendment and the constitution, and yet still stands during those time. This one shares its same idea but was considered to be stricken from the law and considered unconstitutional. Again, I shall state this statement once again, "A state can pass any such legislative measure they see fit just as long as they are not contradicting with the federal constitution."

The Supreme Court of the land has made it also clear that it will strike down any such law that is an unconstitutional act of congress or an act by a state legislature. Well, they never really struck down *Plessy* from the legislative archives and that law was indeed unconstitutional. The court has acted in a hypocritical sense against its American federalism principle. I am glad that this time, this city ordinance, and other ones alike were struck down based on this ruling and saw some equality justice come to our sweet American land of liberty and equality.

"Following the Civil War, certain amendments to the constitution were adopted, which have become an integral part of that instrument, equally binding upon all the states and fixing certain fundamental rights which all are bound

The Amendments

to respect. The Thirteenth Amendment abolished slavery in the United States and in all places subject to jurisdiction, and gave Congress the power to enforce the amendment by appropriate legislation. The Fourteenth Amendment made all persons born or naturalized in the United States, persons of the United States and of the states in which they reside, and provided that no state shall make or enforce any law which shall abridge the privileges or immunities of persons of the United States, and that no state shall deprive any person of life, liberty, or property without due process *76 of law, nor deny to any person the equal protection of the laws." (Opinion Brief of Buchanan v. Warley, Associate Justice William R. Day).

In the case of the slaughterhouse rulings in where these fresh amendments were added to our principled document. The majority of that court made it known that the fourteenth amendment is a protection of the privileges and immunities of citizenship in the United States. Associate Justice Samuel F. Miller, who spoke for the majority of this ruling is absolutely wrong in describing the function of the Fourteenth Amendment. The Fourteenth Amendment is part of the federal Constitution and by being a part of this principled document, states must abide to it with no contradiction. The slaughterhouse case rulings stated that the new amendments added to the Constitution were only there to protect the person of the United States, not the person of each state. This country fought a civil war for racial equality under law for all states. If it is dictated in the constitution, then it applies to all the several and autonomous states.

How can an amendment only apply to the privileges and immunities of persons in the nation but not within the states? Again, the *Plessy* ruling was to please former and descendants of confederate soldiers and politicians to try to maintain the once era known as the antebellum society. Justice Miller

II. The Fourteenth Amendment, 1868

and the rest of that court are wrong and unconstitutional, plain, and simple.

Justice Day in the opinion brief of *Buchanan*, brings up the supreme court case of *Strauder v. West Virginia*. Justice William Strong in speaking for the majority to rise in defense for the Constitution and Fourteenth Amendment.

"It [the Fourteenth Amendment] was designed to assure to the colored race the enjoyment of all the civil rights that under the law are enjoyed by white persons, and to give to that race the protection of the general government, in that enjoyment, whenever it should be denied by the states. It only gave personship and the privileges of personship to persons of color, but it denied to any state the power to withhold from them the equal protection of the laws, and authorized Congress to enforce its provisions by appropriate legislation. It ordains that no state shall deprive any person of life, liberty or property, without due process of law, or deny to any person within its jurisdiction the equal protection of the laws." (Opinion Brief of Buchanan v. Warley, Associate Justice William R. Day).

> "Any state action that denies this immunity
> to a colored man is in conflict with the
> constitution."
>
> Associate Justice William R. Day

As Justice John M. Harlan stated it in *Plessy v. Ferguson*. As Associate Justice William R. Day stated in *Buchanan v. Warley*. Any state that contradicts and is in dire conflict with the federal constitution is wrong. The said state legislation remains to be unconstitutional. The law does not cast privilege under law, it casts equality under law. The Fourteenth Amendment is also quite clear that a state cannot show any hint of favoritism to one race and not to the other race. It must show an equal balance of the law to all races that have taken the oath of citizenship allegiance to the constitution and to their state of residence.

"We think this attempt to prevent the alienation of the property in question to a person of color was not a legitimate exercise of the police power of the state, and is in direct violation of the fundamental law enacted in the Fourteenth Amendment of the Constitution preventing state interference with property rights except by due process of the law. That being the case, the ordinance cannot stand. Booth v. Illinois, 184 U.S. 425, 429, 22 Sup. Ct. 425, 46 L. Ed. 623; **21 Otis v. Parker, 187 U.S. 606, 609, 23 Sup. Ct. 168, 47 L. 323. Reaching this conclusion it follows that the judgment of the Kentucky Court of Appeals must be reversed, and the cause remanded to that court for further proceedings not inconsistent with this opinion. Reversed." (Opinion Brief of Buchanan v. Warley, Associate Justice William R. Day).

I have read multiple opinions of the Supreme Court of the United States and I truly have to say in reading this particular ruling has made me proud to be called an American and a follower of the American federalism principle. The Supreme Court has taken a giant leap for equality and to remind the states the whole issue of federalism. The autonomous and sovereign states of this republic can establish any legislation for that state. But let that legislation in question show no conflict or contradiction towards the federal constitution of this new, reshaped republic. That is the true principle of the American federalism republic. I stand with the majority of this ruling, for the rule of the Constitution and for the rule of equality to continue to flourish among our reshaped republic. The high court stated that residential segregation was unconstitutional, and people would have stopped this unfair practice. But the sad reality is that because do not

II. The Fourteenth Amendment, 1868

read with high court rulings and do not educate themselves, residential segregation, and segregation itself continued to cause rampage across our land.

* * *

After *Buchanan v. Warley* in 1917, we all believed that the unconstitutional idea of "separate but equal" precedent would phase would just fade away. We were all mistaken, and the country continued to be in conflict and in contradiction with the federal constitution. It would not be till 1954, thirty-seven years later that the supreme court had to reiterate their decision on the racial question on the side of liberty and equality, and the Constitution. It's final nail to the unconstitutional coffin in 1967.

The issue of classifying residential segregation to be unconstitutional did not stop there to bring all persons to be equal under the law. School segregation was the next target to bring a clear definition of the Fourteenth Amendment's equality and liberty clause. The target of bringing an end to segregation in private accommodations came later with the passage of the congressional action of the 1964 Civil Rights Act.

The threat of school segregation did not only affect in the southern states. It affected it all across these states of this American union.

I remember a small anecdote that a dear friend, Jack M. Wells from Neihart, Montana once told me while he was in school in the 1940s and 1950s. His school up in Great Falls, Montana was indeed segregated with white children and Native American children. As he told me the story, when his class broke for recess and they were playing outside. Jack noticed some children in the basement of the school…he then asked his teacher, "Who were those children?" The teacher responded, "Those children are Native Indians, and they will be out for recess after you finished with your recess." To that Jack replied very innocently, "I want to play with these children", and the teacher stated it was not possible. I remember these words from Jack Moore Wells, that he could not tolerate injustice and cruelty, just because of the color of their skin. Even in Big Sky Country there was the policy of 'separate but equal,' among white persons and Native American persons.

Segregation was everywhere and it was treated as a normal American way of life but as we all know it was not normal and it was quite unconstitutional.

"*Mendez v. Westminster* (1947) was a school desegregation case involving students of Mexican ancestry. Federal judge Paul McCormick, a Coolidge appointee, based his decision on strict construction of California law and on the Fourteenth's Amendment equal protection clause." (Race & Liberty in America, The Essential Reader, Classical Liberals in the Civil Rights Era Edited by Jonathan Bean, The Independent Institute, The University Press of Kentucky, 2009, p. 187).

Even though, it was a state issue, the federal court in California accepted the Constitution as it is written for equality under law for all persons. But, unfortunately, there was little impact for equality for persons of Mexican descent and blacks in the sovereign state of California. Then-governor Earl Warren signed a bill entitled "The Anderson Bill" in 1947 outlawing segregation only where it was not legal. During this time in California had laws sanctioning segregation of Native Americans and Asians. Also, unfortunately, this legislation did continue the segregation against black-Americans.

In 1954, there was a ruling that once again brought up the issue of "separate but equal" in our educational institutions. This issue should have been buried almost forty years ago

II. The Fourteenth Amendment, 1868

but this time, the issue of racial equality was addressed in the education system of our states. The case of *Brown v. Board of Education* showed the American federalism point of view that the courts interpret the law as it is written and if it is agreeing with the constitution. This court ruling finally sealed the fate of the unconstitutional ruling and despicable way of life that was governing unjustly for all our citizenry. The court decision was unanimous because all the jurists agreed that it was the right thing to do to show the rest of the country and the world, that the American federalism principle is alive and well and that states cannot contradict federal constitutional law.

"We conclude that in the field of public education the doctrine of 'separate but equal' has no place. Therefore, we hold that the plaintiffs and other similarly situated for whom the actions have been brought are, by reason of segregation complained of, deprived of the equal protection of the laws guaranteed by the Fourteenth Amendment. This disposition makes unnecessary any discussion whether such segregation also violates the Due Process Clause of the Fourteenth Amendment. It is so ordered." (Opinion Brief of Brown v. Board of Education, 1954, Chief Justice Earl Warren).

The Supreme Court in this 1954 ruling finally laid down the constitution and rule of law that the idea of 'separate but equal' began, continued, and ended as an unconstitutional idea. As the middle of the twentieth century was a beginning, a new era of civil rights began to arise and now the American citizenry from across the country was not going to tolerate any more unconstitutionality from their state legislators and bureaucrats.

This 1954 ruling finally took over and stood up that it was time to end this ridiculous idea that the East Louisiana Railway concocted in their state with strict contradiction to

The Amendments

the federal constitution. Although some states, particularly kept disobeying a federal court ruling and the constitution but now the central government given the authority by congress was not going to tolerate it anymore. The beginning of the end of racial inequality and discrimination was at an end but in the meantime, a new form of racial inequality was rising with also no constitutional basis. This new form of racial inequality took the stand in the supreme court chamber in 1989 where Associate Justice Scalia showed again his rightful and federalism colors in interpreting the constitution in how it is supposed to be interpreted. There is supposed to be no racial inequality of any shape or form, and it goes against the Constitution.

As I said in the beginning in discussing the Fourteenth Amendment regarding race relations. This union may be legally and lawfully integrated with full accordance of the law, but emotionally, we are still unfortunately a divided union of sovereign states.

"The State of South Carolina came in and admitted that those inequalities existed and declared its intention to remove them as promptly as possible. Evidence was taken; the district court decreed that the Constitution and statute of South Carolina did not violate the Amendment; found the existence of the admitted inequality, and enjoined its immediate removal, gave the State of South Carolina the period of six months to report what steps had taken to implement that decree." (Oral Argument of John W. Davis, Esq., on behalf of Appellees R.W. Elliot et al., Brown v. Board of Education, 1954).

If the state of South Carolina did submit that inequalities did exist in the different schools within that state. Then they did not look harder and failed miserably. Their bureaucratic education system failed miserably towards all persons of their fine state. Also, if the state of South Carolina had taken

II. The Fourteenth Amendment, 1868

the immediate steps to rectify the inequality...we all missed those advisories to fix these steps.

John W. Davis was a definite supporter of the movement for the state sovereign doctrine for segregation, not only in schools but every aspect of American life. His family were originally from Virginia, but when a portion of that state seceded from Virginia, the family moved to West Virginia. He ran for president in the Democratic ticket in 1924. He lost to the republican incumbent president Calvin Coolidge and more importantly, Coolidge obtained the black vote. But that did not stop Davis to continue his racist rant for segregated and unconstitutional policies across this union.

Davis just did not quite comprehend in how this American union of sovereign states works and was established. He goes on in his unruly and unprincipled oral argument of racism to criticize and mock the Pennsylvanian abolitionist national representative Thaddeus Stevens, the man behind the authorship of the Fourteenth Amendment.

"In the House, Thaddeus Stevens, called by historians perhaps the most unlovely character in American history, more concerned to humiliate the aristocrats in the South, as he called them, even than to preserve the rights of the Negro. His policy was confiscation of all estates over 10,000 dollars and 200 acres, of which forty dollars should be given to every adult Negro, and the remainder should be sold to pay the expenses of the war. He wanted the South to come to Washington as suppliants in sackcloth and ashes. He has his echoes." (Oral Argument of John W. Davis, Esq., on behalf of Appellees R.W. Elliot et al., Brown v. Board of Education, 1954).

"More concerned to humiliate the aristocrats in the South." I will tell you something, the southern aristocrats could not care less for the middle-class ancestry of the Davis family. For him to stand up for the once-upper-class families of the

The Amendments

various southern states to prove a racist and ridiculous point is beyond absurd. The amendment that Davis may be talking about was the Thirteenth Amendment, to abolish the labor force known as slavery. But as the newly freed people were trying to make a decent life after years of forced bondage, the re-patriated state legislatures decided to crush their liberty and freedoms by keeping them in the fields. Even though, they were not slaves, been paid little, you could say that slavery was still in existence.

So, Representative Stevens and his abolitionist compatriots decided to extend the sense of liberty with the newly added Fourteenth Amendment to show equality for all persons, includes both white, black, etc.

The matter on the table discussion was to bring an end to this ridiculous compromise of 'separate, but equal' that is a far-off compromise than the Missouri Compromise. To bring an end of the injustices in the education system of the various states in the south and west that had an unconstitutional and racist tirade point of view was a good cause to end it. The black schools were not as advanced as the white schools in schooling materials and curriculum, so the sense of "separate but equal" was a hypocritical mindset.

"Mr. Davis, would not the necessary and proper clause apply to the Amendment as well as to the enumerated powers of the instrument itself? In other words, if Congress should say that in order to accomplish the purposes of equality in the other fields, the abolition of segregation was necessary, as a necessary and proper clause?" (Oral Argument Question of Associate Justice Robert Jackson on R.W. Elliot et al., Brown v. Board of Education, 1954).

"Well, if you can imagine a necessary and proper clause which would enforce the provisions of this article by dealing with matter which is not within the scope of the article itself, which I think is a contradiction in terms, that is a

II. The Fourteenth Amendment, 1868

paradox. Congress could do what the Amendment did not warrant under the guise of enforcing the Amendment." (Oral Argument of John W. Davis, Esq., on behalf of Appellees R.W. Elliot et al., Brown v. Board of Education, 1954).

I will tell you what is in contradiction in term…the very thought of an idea to be 'separate, but equal,' because it showed no equality while separated. While white schools got better educative tools for the white children…the black schools are disparaged and denied getting those same tools.

Yes, I do believe that it is necessary and proper for Congress to use these tools to enforce the said Amendment, especially when it is written in Section V of the Amendment.

> Section V. The Congress shall have power to enforce, by appropriate legislation, the provisions of this article.

This happens when the ordinary American that truly lacks common sense failed to read and comprehend the Constitution and all its articles. Therefore, we have the racial problems that we have now because ignorance travels fast than common sense. It is within Congress' duty to act with necessary and proper use of their authority to enforce any person being mistreated against the law and shown any inequality of the law.

The Supreme Court already made it clear that one aspect of segregation in residential neighborhoods to be unconstitutional. And yet, the emotionality among the ignorant mind ran rampart than the common sense of the constitutionalist mind.

The Constitution can be changed to better the hearts and minds of all individuals living in this republic. The constitutional framers were not perfect men, but they knew that their heirs to the republic would see fit to continue reshaping the republic to continue its glory for liberty and freedom. The glory of liberty, freedom, and equality that is embedded in the Declaration of Independence and in the Constitution's bill of rights.

But, unfortunately, there were individuals that were too emotional at heart to an old southern way of life, some probably does not have lavish stories from their ancestors living in an aristocratic life. But others, after the war were so bitter of this loss that they would do anything in their power to prevent the rights and liberties of the new freed persons and be a constitutional obstacle to the legislations of the federal government.

Then, unfortunately, we will have not only right-wing contradictions to the constitution. But left-wing contradictions to the constitution and that will lead to more anger and distrust of our founding document with these added amendments and governing bodies.

The decision of *Brown v. Board of Education* was agreed unanimously to end racial discrimination upon all schools across our union. It also decreed that it partially ended the uncouth and unconstitutional judicial decree of 'separate but equal' on our schools.

* * *

Modern-day statesmen and legislators accessing and interpreting this Fourteenth Article has been quite disheartening to bring forth divisions and chaos to our newly reshaped American republic.

We have had multiple civil rights legislations under the guidance of the Fourteenth Amendment, but never too much to hold enforcement power. As Martin Luther King, Jr., once said that then-Senate Majority leader Lyndon B. Johnson

II. The Fourteenth Amendment, 1868

gutted the 1957 civil rights bill "was like soup made from bones of an emaciated chicken."

Then came the legislative battle of the enaction of the 1964 civil rights bill. The proposed bill had good intentions but overbearing and extreme funding extremities from the federal government. The challenging aspect of the fight for equal civil rights is to set and be rid of the established contradictory rule of 'separate but equal' ruling in schools and other accommodations, public and private.

"The intentions of the Fourteenth Amendment's authors are perfectly clear. Consider these facts. 1) During the entire congressional debate of the Fourteenth Amendment it was never once suggested by any proponent of the amendment that it would outlaw segregated schools. 2) At the time that it approved the Fourteenth Amendment, Congress established schools in Washington in Georgetown "for the sole use of... colored children." 3. In all the debates on the amendment by the state legislatures there was only one legislator in Indiana, who thought the amendment would affect schools. 4. The great majority of the States that approved the amendment permitted or required segregated schools at the very time they approved the amendment... The amendment was not intended to, and therefore it did not outlaw racially segregated schools." (The Conscience of a Conservative, Goldwater, Barry M., Regnery Gateway, 1990, p. 29).

As I have much respect for the esteemed gentleman senator of Arizona for all his convictions and opinions that he may have introduced on the senate floor. He is quite wrong on the issue of liberty and equality when it came to the Fourteenth Amendment. Indeed, the framers of this amendment could not foresee and predict the terrible ordeal this union would undergo to create this separation and inequality across our nation's schools, both public and private.

The Amendments

Tell it to the national Congress to divide a union to please one group with privilege and deny it to another. Why did Congress have to establish a colored-only school in the Georgetown area? The federal government gives this type of incentive, then the sovereign states will look upon it as it is an alright legal gesture to create these types of inequality institutions.

If the supreme court would not have interpreted the Fourteenth Amendment with the doctrine of 'separate but equal'. Then we would not have seen the terrible ordeals of inequality and violence throughout this union. If this high court would have given the authority, pre-civil war, for all states to enforce the constitution as they see fit without encouraging privilege. Then this nation would be the union of sovereign states that the original framers intended to create. But it is what it is now, and now we must keep reshaping this republic to create the equality the framers of this amendment created under the guidance of the constitution.

"States' rights are easy to define. The Tenth Amendment does it succinctly." (The Conscience of a Conservative, Goldwater, Barry M., Regnery Gateway, 1990, p.26).

It is the distinct duty of a sovereign state's right to define the laws as instructed in the Constitution. But when a sovereign state refuses to define and write laws that are in contradiction to the Constitution or goes along to an unprincipled and unconstitutional ruling of the high court. It is self-evident that we are dealing with ignorant members of our lawful society of this republic. This nation has dealt with this kind of ignorance before, our American union had to go to a civil war due because of this ignorance. To continue with the same level of constitutional ignorance and not evolved to correctly reshape our republic's founding document is troubling.

II. The Fourteenth Amendment, 1868

Plus, we have a Ninth Amendment before the Tenth Amendment. Our rights are defined by the individual, not by a state entity.

"It was not intended to, and therefore it did not, authorize any federal intervention in the field of education." (The Conscience of a Conservative, Goldwater, Barry M., Regnery Gateway, 1990, p.29-30).

Then it is intended for the federal government as instructed in Section V of the Fourteenth Amendment to enforce this amendment with the appropriate legislation. It is not an invasion of state sovereignty. The states still retain their sovereignty if they do it in the lawful fashion to enact laws with constitutional accordance under the Fourteenth. Under the guidance of an unprincipled high court ruling in 1896, and then in 1954, the high court saw the wisdom to notice the unprincipled ruling to correct it with the right principle. Then it is the duty of Congress to instruct the federal executive branch to enforce it appropriately...as dictated in Section V. This only should come to effect if the states refuse to define Amendment Fourteen with the proper constitutional enforcement.

"A civil right is a right that is asserted and is therefore protected by some valid law. It may be asserted by the common law, or by local or federal statutes, or by the Constitution; but unless a right is incorporated in the law, it is not a civil right and is not enforceable by the instruments of the civil law. There may be some rights— "natural," "human," or otherwise—that should also be civil rights. But if we desire to give such rights the protection of the law, our recourse is to a legislature or to the amendment procedures of the Constitution. We must not look to politicians, or sociologists—or the courts—to correct the deficiency." (The Conscience of a Conservative, Goldwater, Barry M., Regnery Gateway, 1990, p.26-27).

The Amendments

Civil rights and liberties were given onto us by our constitutional framers in the beginning of this constitution's 1787 adoption. And when this union's national Congress want to reinforce our bill of rights into one amendment, it is up to righteous and constitutionally principled national politicians to create, amend and reshape the republic for us the sovereign states' principled politicians to enforce it.

> "We must not look to politicians, or sociologists—or the courts—to correct the deficiency."
> – Barry Goldwater.

This statement is awfully contradictory and goes against our rules of federalism and constitution. If we do not look upon the politicians to make the laws and amendments in accordance with our constitution. Then who do we look upon...an arrogant federal chief executive? If it was the courts that took us into a path of constitutional contradictions and unprincipled rulings...then who can correct them but the national politicians within the national Congress? It is a power now invested within the national government that it is what it is now dictated. The court can see a wrong and correct it and that is what they did in 1954 and 1967 and later in 1989.

> "Our Constitution guarantees equal rights to all our persons, without discrimination on account of race and color. I have taken my oath to support that Constitution."
> – Calvin Coolidge

In this American union of sovereign states, we must look upon the Constitution, original and additions, and we must find a way to cope with one another to bring liberty and equality

II. The Fourteenth Amendment, 1868

under the law and peace with our fellow persons of all races, creeds, and sex. As a great former president of this American republic of sovereign states once stated that he took the constitutional oath to protect and enforce that all persons are equal under law. All equal under law with no sense of discrimination on account of race or color (and sex), and this means all.

* * *

Years ago, an incredibly good friend and former employer of mine asked me if I supported affirmative action. And my response to that question was. "If people would just have read the Constitution, the Fourteenth Amendment. Then we would not have had affirmative action.

'Separate but equal', and 'affirmative action' are quite the contradictions to the Constitution. Our principled document does not share the principle of privilege under law for a specific race or color or sex of people and deny it others. Our principled document shares the principle of equality under law for all our persons, male, and female of all races… plain and simple.

"In Grutter v. Bollinger, 2003, as the senior justice in the majority of five voting to uphold the University of Michigan Law School's affirmative action program, I wisely assigned the majority opinion to Sandra Day O'Connor. In that opinion, she squarely held that the law school had a compelling interest in attaining a diverse student body." (The Making of a Justice: Reflections on My First 94 Years, Justice Paul Stevens, Little Brown and Company, 2019, p. 398).

"Three aspects of that message merit special comment— its legal reasoning, its historical context, and the prestige of its authors." (The Making of a Justice: Reflections on My First 94 Years, Justice Paul Stevens, Little Brown and Company, 2019, p. 399).

The Amendments

"The brief recounted the transition from a segregated to an integrated military. Within a few years after President Truman's 1948 executive order abolishing segregation in the armed forces, the enlisted ranks were fully integrated." (The Making of a Justice: Reflections on My First 94 Years, Justice Paul Stevens, Little Brown and Company, 2019, p. 399).

A school, whether public or private must have a quite diverse student body to ensure that all our liberties and sense of all discrimination does not contaminate the school's student body.

"Sandra went on to conclude that "[e]ffective participation by members of all racial and ethnic groups in the civic life of our Nation is essential if the dream of one Nation, indivisible, is to be realized." (The Making of a Justice: Reflections on My First 94 Years, Justice Paul Stevens, Little Brown and Company, 2019, p. 400).

"After concluding that the law school had permissibly used race as a factor contributing to diversity, Sandra acknowledged that a core purpose of the Fourteenth Amendment was to do away with all discrimination based on race, and therefore that "race-conscious admissions policies must be limited in time." (The Making of a Justice: Reflections on My First 94 Years, Justice Paul Stevens, Little Brown and Company, 2019, p. 401).

But to show government enforcement to topple down merit with misguided sense of equality by force is not why the Fourteenth Amendment was established in the first place. Yes, President Truman abolished segregation in our American union's armed forces. That was a rightful and dutiful thing to do to reshape our republic based on the Fourteenth's true and correct interpretation. The armed forces had a separate but equal way of army living during those days. Many black Americans served in the armed forces, under segregation but some obtained a change in the ranks with the sense of merit, under separated unconstitutional circumstances.

II. The Fourteenth Amendment, 1868

The integration welcomed for a new merit status for all Americans to serve one another with no sense of racism or bigotry. But the merit was not removed by forced with the misguided of false equality. I rather follow the Constitution and a high officer like Colin Powell than a high officer like Robert E. Lee.

I conclude that an effective participation by all members of all racial and ethnic groups, from whites, from blacks, from Hispanics, from Asians, and from Native Americans are to have a prominent civic life within our nation to endure it with equality. Denying merit on a basis of equality is not the true meaning of the Fourteenth Amendment.

The Virginia Military Institute (VMI) is a public institution that receives government funds. That is a clear sign that all persons, citizens, and non-citizens should be treated equally under law. If anybody wishes to attend this public-funded institution, they have every right to register and attend. Female individuals should indeed not be discriminated based on their sex because with accordance of their Bill of Rights. Person individuals based on their race or color, also protected under their bill of rights, and affirmed by the Fourteenth Amendment.

- Parties who seek to defend gender-based government action must demonstrate an "exceedingly persuasive justification" for that action.

    (Opinion of the Court of United States v. Virginia, by Associate Justice Ruth B. Ginsburg, 1996).

There is an extended persuasive justification of a constitutional violation towards the female persons residing in this union. But that clear persuasive justification is founded in the Bill of Rights. It is not founded in the Equal Protection Clause of the Fourteenth Amendment.

- Virginia's categorical exclusion of women from the educational opportunities VMI provides denies equal protection to women.

    (Opinion of the Court of United States v. Virginia, by Associate Justice Ruth B. Ginsburg, 1996).

We should not have any exclusion from any publicly funded institutions or privately-publicly funded institutions for any kind of persons residing in our union. Because our Constitution's Bill of Rights forbid it. The late Justice Ruth Bader Ginsburg was quite the intellectual American individual, but sometimes residing with emotions in her opinions and not with her common-sense mind. The thinking of Ginsburg is similar to those in 1857 and 1896 filled with emotions.

- The remedy proffered by Virginia-maintain VMI as a male-only college and create VWIL as a separate program for women-does not cure the constitutional violation.

    (Opinion of the Court of United States v. Virginia, by Associate Justice Ruth B. Ginsburg, 1996).

"The VWIL program is a pale shadow of VMI in terms of the range of curricular choices and faculty stature, funding, prestige, alumni support and influence." (Opinion of the Court of United States v. Virginia, by Associate Justice Ruth B. Ginsburg, 1996).

Justice Ginsburg is rightly in putting that creating a 'separate but equal' standard for male and female cadets casts a deep (bigoted) shadow on the institution. She is prescribing the wrong perception into this judgment. There is clearly a constitutional violation among some publicly funded

II. The Fourteenth Amendment, 1868

institutions, but it is not under a Fourteenth Amendment violation.

Would Justice Ginsburg have casted the same majority opinion if this case were brought up in United States v. Mt. Holyoke College? Yes, Mt. Holyoke is a private college, yet they receive and have received federal funding and grants, ideally making them a Government Sponsored Entity. So, I repeat the question, would Justice Ginsburg cast a similar majority opinion.

The great second dissenter of our high court speaks with great constitutional volumes. Justice Antonin Scalia was the lone dissenter regarding the case of *United States v. Virginia* and had lots to say to Justice Ginsburg's majority opinion. Everybody was aware of the great friendship between Scalia and Ginsburg. Even great friendships come with a little feud. But that is the perfect friendship where they remain friends, while agreeing to disagree on important issues of our nation as guaranteed in our first amendment.

"(I)f the question of the applicable standard of review for sex-based classifications were to be regarded as an appropriate subject for reconsideration, the stronger argument would be not for elevating the standard to strict scrutiny, but for reducing it to rational-basis review." (Dissenting Opinion of the Court of United States v. Virginia, by Associate Justice Antonin Scalia, 1996).

Justice Scalia believed in equality under law, but within the appropriate defining of those rights. There is frankly no equal protection clause under the Fourteenth Amendment for sex-based classifications. The Fourteenth Amendment was an affirmation to the bill of rights to extend to race and color relations across this American union of sovereign states. It did not extend to sex and same-sex affirmations. Those are rested in our Ten bill of rights exclusively, especially in the Ninth. It is stated all citizens, male, and female, have the same rights and protections of Constitution's bill of rights, but not in the Fourteenth Amendment.

For publicly funded institutions to create a 'separate but equal" policy for male and female cadets is idiotic and quite contradictory as if it were a 'separate but equal' for white and black cadets. It must be applied correctly on the appropriate legislation or amendment. A violation of 'separate but equal' within male and female cadets' rests on the initial bill of rights challenge; sixth, seventh, and ninth. A violation of 'separate but equal" within the white and black cadets' rests on a Fourteenth Amendment challenge.

We all sympathize with the injustices of what the black community has endured. But to apply a 'reverse racism' platform is plainly not dictated in the Fourteenth Amendment.

* * *

The dissenting opinion of the case *Richmond v. J.A. Croson Co.* is just as unconstitutional as the majority opinion of *Plessy v. Ferguson.*

The city council of the city of Richmond, Virginia, was once the centralized government location capital city of the Confederate States of America. You would be surprised what the city council members proposed to the city in its new program for awarding municipal contracts.

Let us all remember that in the height of the established unconstitutional rebellion nation-state, the capital of this new nation moved their seat in national government from Montgomery, Alabama to Richmond, Virginia. Things had changed in that city long after the civil war when General Ulysses Grant bombarded the city, the ugly days of unconstitutional segregation. That city was a small black sheep of cities within the Commonwealth of Virginia.

II. The Fourteenth Amendment, 1868

"To hide their racist shortcomings of their past, the city council adopted a Minority Business Utilization Plan (Plan) requiring prime contractors awarded city construction contracts to subcontract at 30% of the dollar amount of each contract to one or more "Minority Business Enterprises" (MBE's), which the Plan defined to include a business from anywhere in the country at least 51% of which is owned and controlled by black, Spanish-speaking, Oriental, Indian, Eskimo, or Aleut persons. The proposal was adopted after a public hearing at which no direct evidence was presented that the city had discriminated on the basis of race in letting contracts or that its prime contractors had discriminated against minority subcontractors. The city's plan was presented as constitutional under *Fullilove v. Klutznick*." (Syllabus of Richmond v. J.A. Croson Co ruling, 1989).

This is usual of former cities of the old south that once engaged in racial inequality and racial discrimination before, during, and after the civil war. The majority of the white population felt guilty to what their ancestors did during the antebellum days and present grandparents did during the segregation days, and so they thought they would correct the wrong by applying something to be believed to be good, and yet still unconstitutional as simple racism. 'Reverse racism' may sound with good intentions but remains with unconstitutional intentions.

Racism and placing discriminatory acts against an individual of color is wrong and unconstitutional. But using 'reverse racism' for the opposite for non-white individuals is the same act of discrimination.

But while they apply reverse racism, they bring up the same unconstitutionality of Judge Leon M. Bazile, the judge that unjustly sentenced the Loving couple. The interracial couple that ended the prohibition of mixed-racial marriages.

The Amendments

"It is a welcome symbol of racial progress when the former capital of the Confederacy acts forthrightly to confront the effects of racial discrimination in its midst. In my view, nothing in the Constitution can be construed to prevent Richmond, Virginia, from allocating a portion of its contracting dollars for businesses owned or controlled by members of minority groups. Indeed, Richmond's set-aside program is indistinguishable in all meaningful respects from—and in fact which this court upheld in *Fullilove v. Klutznick*." (Dissenting Opinion of Richmond v. J.A. Croson Co ruling, Associate Justice Thurgood Marshall, 1989).

No matter what happened in those old cities of the south, north, east, or west of the United States, the civil war amendments stood that there would be no discrimination for all races. When the Fourteenth Amendment meant 'all races', it meant for black, white, native American, Eskimo, etc. I understand why Associate Justice Thurgood Marshall dissented and that is because he was a man that saw a lot of injustices for the black American community.

"We all sympathize with the injustices of what the black community endured, but to apply a 'reverse racism' platform is plainly not dictated in the Fourteenth Amendment."

But what is even more terrible to practice is reverse racism to be a form of vengeance to create an illusion of applied law with false information that there were minority-owned companies that faced discriminations. But as we read into the opinion of the court and the concurrence of Associate Justice Antonin Scalia, we see that is false and misconstrued information. The workforce of this union is based on merit, not on privilege for some races, and not all.

II. The Fourteenth Amendment, 1868

"1. The city has failed to demonstrate a compelling governmental interest justifying the Plan, since the factual predicate supporting the Plan does not establish the type of identified past discrimination in the city's construction industry that would authorize race-based relief under the Fourteenth Amendment's Equal Protection Clause." (Opinion of Richmond v. J.A. Croson Co ruling, Associate Justice Sandra Day O'Connor, 1989).

"The "evidence" relied upon by Justice MARSHALL's dissent—the city's history of school desegregation and numerous congressional reports—does little to define the scope of any injury to minority contractors in the city or the necessary remedy, and could justify a preference of any size or duration. Moreover, Justice MARSHALL's suggestion that discrimination findings may be "shared" from jurisdiction to jurisdiction is unprecedented and contrary to this Court's decisions." (Opinion of Richmond v. J.A. Croson Co ruling, Associate Justice Sandra Day O'Connor, 1989).

What does the issue of school segregation in the City of Richmond have anything to do with companies trying or not trying to discriminate minority-owned contracting businesses? Absolutely nothing, sadly, Justice Marshall is fishing at the bottom of the barrel trying to clear up the city of Richmond from their stench shameful history of slavery and segregation and so he would dictate an orchestrated lie to satisfy a new wave of supposed anti-discrimination for that city. Let us dig in a little deeper into Marshall's dissent and see if truly we can find better concrete evidence of discrimination by the City of Richmond that does not include segregation discrimination in the Richmond school system.

I do have to say that Justice Day O'Connor's opinion shows some flimsy, topsy-turvy opinions, stating that the city cannot provide past racial discriminations and yet they state that it can with the usage of the Fourteenth Amendment's

The Amendments

Equal Protection Clause. They state that they could route out racial discrimination by race-based legislation by the General Assembly of the Commonwealth of Virginia. As I have stated before, states can pass any form legislation that they see fit as long as it is not in conflict and contradicting to the federal constitution. Having the state legislature of a state pass anti-racial based legislation/s. It must protect all races against discrimination. The state law cannot nit-pick what race to cover and what race not to cover, that is where I differ from Justice Marshall's dissent.

Justice Antonin Scalia filed a concurrence opinion apart from the opinion and I am glad he did because he is more of a true constitutional jurist to stick to our American federalism principle than Justice Day O'Connor. And so, I keep applauding this man and wish we could have more jurists like that in the high court.

"I agree with much of the Court's opinion, and, in particular, with Justice O'CONNOR's conclusion that strict scrutiny must be applied to all governmental classification **736 by race, whether or not its asserted purpose is "remedial" or "benign." Ante, at 721—722. I do not agree, however, with Justice O'CONNOR's dictum suggesting that, despite the Fourteenth Amendment, state and local governments may in some circumstances discriminate on the basis of race in order (in a broad sense) "to ameliorate the effects of past discrimination." (Concurrence Opinion of Richmond v. J.A. Croson Co ruling, Associate Justice Antonin Scalia, 1989).

In reading Justice Scalia's opening concurrence statement, he reminds me of Justice John Marshall Harlan's dissent on *Plessy v. Ferguson*. Strictly constitutional and not emotional at heart. What Scalia is stating is that communities across the states cannot pick and choose the race to defend. It was wrong to nit-pick during the reconstruction era all through

II. The Fourteenth Amendment, 1868

the segregation era and now it is wrong to reverse a federal article to please one racial group. It was wrong that for many years this union showed privilege to the white race of this republic, but that error has been corrected. This union is based on equality under law, not privilege under law. And we continue to strive to reshape our republic for the sense of liberty.

Anti-constitutionalists have always loved to twist and turn other court rulings to satisfy their special interest agenda instead of a constitutional agenda.

"In *Fullilove v. Klutznick*, 448 U.S. 448, 100Ct. 2758, 65 L. Ed. 2d 902 (1980), we upheld legislative action by Congress similar in its asserted purpose to that at issue here. And we have permitted federal courts to prescribe quite severe race-conscious remedies when confronted with egregious and persistent unlawful discrimination, see, e.g., *United States v. Paradise*, 149, 107 S. Ct. 1053, 94 L.Ed2nd 203 (1987); *Sheet Metal Workers v. EEOC*, 478 U.S. 421, 106 S. Ct. 3019, 92 L.Ed2nd 344 (1986). As Justice OCONNOR acknowledges, however, *ante*, at 717-720 it is one thing to permit racially based conduct by the Federal Government—whose legislative powers concerning matters of race were explicitly enhanced by the Fourteenth Amendment, see U.S. Const., Amdt. 14, Sec 5—and quite another permit by the precise entities against whose conduct in *522 matters of race that Amendment was specifically directed, see Amdt. 14, Sec 1. As we said in *Ex parte Virginia supra*, 100 U.S., at 345, the Civil War Amendments were designed to "take away all possibility of oppression by law because of race or color" and "to be ... limitations on the power of the States and enlargements of *737 the power of Congress." (Concurrence Opinion of Richmond v. J.A. Croson Co ruling, Associate Justice Antonin Scalia, 1989).

The Amendments

One who may read this partial statement from Scalia's Concurrence opinion may think that he is for an overly powerful central government, but nothing could be further from the truth. He was a constitutional realist and knew specifically why the Civil War Amendments were added to the federal Constitution. States cannot disavow and create conflict with federal constitutional amendments. Especially after they indeed have ratified them.

"In my view there is only one circumstance in which the States may act by race to "undo the effects of past discrimination": where that is necessary to eliminate their own maintenance of a system of unlawful racial classification. If, for example, a state agency has a discriminatory pay scale compensating black employees in all positions at 20% less than their nonblack counterparts, it may assuredly promulgate an order raising the salaries of "all black employees" to eliminate the differential." (Concurrence Opinion of Richmond v. J.A. Croson Co ruling, Associate Justice Antonin Scalia, 1989).

What Scalia is stating in not being a right-wing nationalist or left-wing progressive centrist. He is plainly advocating for state sovereignty and still maintaining the American federalism principles bestowed by our constitutional framers and by the Fourteenth Amendment framers. States must abide the federal constitution to create their own laws. Their enforcement must coincide with the ratified amendments, and one slight contradiction to that effect, results and has resulted in federal executive enforcement via-congressional oversight. Also, in reading part of Scalia's Concurrence opinion, he mentions our father of the constitution, James Madison. James Madison was a staunch state sovereignty advocate while maintaining the American federalism principle alive.

II. The Fourteenth Amendment, 1868

"As James Madison observed in support of the proposed Constitution's enhancement of national powers:" "The smaller the society, the fewer probably will be the distinct parties, and interests composing it; the fewer the distinct parties and interests, the more frequently will a majority be found of the same party; and the smaller the number of individuals composing a majority, and the smaller the compass within which they are placed, the more easily will they concert and execute their plan of oppression. Extend the sphere and you take in a greater variety of parties and interests; you make it less probable that a majority of the whole will have a common motive to invade the rights of other persons; or if such a common motive exists, it will be more difficult for all who feel it to discover their own strength and to act in unison with each other." The Federalist No., 10, pp. 82-84 (C. Rossiter ed. 1961). (Concurrence Opinion of Richmond v. J.A. Croson Co ruling, Associate Justice Antonin Scalia, 1989).

What James Madison is saying in Federalist #10, is that when a small sect of the community gets together, they will do more harm to the principles of the government. While the other persons because they are out for a personal vindictive agenda rather than creating laws to benefit all persons. In this case, the Civil War Amendments did just that to satisfy all persons based on race.

The amendment in question in this ruling is quite clear, "All races must be treated equally". It does not state, white races equally and colored races unequal, vice-versa. All races are equal under law. We cannot give privilege under law to one race and deny it to another.

"Since I believe that the appellee here had a constitutional right to have its bid succeed or fail under a decision-making process uninfected with racial bias, I concur in the judgment

The Amendments

of the Court." (Concurrence Opinion of Richmond v. J.A. Croson Co ruling, Associate Justice Antonin Scalia, 1989).
I long since concur with Scalia's concurrence opinion than of the opinion of the court. It speaks volumes of the federal constitutional amendment but more than that it speaks volumes of our American federalism principle to reshape our republic with the same structure it began in 1787.
"We stated that the Constitution requires a State "to steer clear, not only of operating the old dual system of racially segregated schools, but also of giving significant aid to institutions that practice racial or other invidious discrimination." "In *Bradley v. School Board of Richmond*, 462 F.2d 1058, 1060, n. (CA4 1972), aff'd by an equally divided Court, **545** 412 U.S. 92, 93 S. Ct. 1952, 36 L.Ed.2d 771 (1973), the Court of Appeals for the Fourth Circuit, sitting en banc, reviewed in the context of a school desegregation case Richmond's long history of inadequate compliance with *Brown v. Board of Education*, 374 U.S. 483, 74 S.Ct. 686, 98 L.Ed. 873 (1954), and the cases implementing its holding. (Dissenting Opinion of Richmond v. J.A. Croson Co ruling, Associate Justice Thurgood Marshall, 1989).
"The dissenting judge elaborated: 'The sordid history of Virginia's and Richmond's attempts to circumvent, defeat, and nullify the holding of *Brown I* has been recorded in the opinions of this and other courts, and need not be repeated in detail here. It suffices to say ****749** that there was massive resistance and every state resource, including the services of private counsel (costing the State hundreds of thousands of Dollars), the State police, and the power and prestige of the Governor, was employed to defeat *Brown I*. In Richmond, as has been mentioned, not even freedom of choice became actually effective until 1966, twelve years after the decision of Brown I.' 462 F.2nd, at 1075 (Winter, J.) (emphasis in

II. The Fourteenth Amendment, 1868

original) (footnotes and citations omitted). (Dissenting Opinion of Richmond v. J.A. Croson Co ruling, Associate Justice Thurgood Marshall, 1989).

No one in the modern constitutional legal scholar world believes that segregated communities were alright and constitutional. It was wrong during the antebellum days and extremely wrong during the days of segregation. But if you are fighting for equality for one race, you cannot disparage the other. The City of Richmond, Virginia, to cover for their racist shortcomings presented to their city council, a policy of reverse racism that is just as unconstitutional as the 'separate but equal' policy. Justice Marshall can be and has all the right to be over-protective in giving the black American community for a leg up. But you should not give a leg up to one race and put down the other race. Marshall's attitude toward this dissent reminds me of the old high court justices and politicians that put the white-American community on a leg up while putting down the black-American community down. That racism was wrong, and the reverse of it is also wrong.

"In short, there is simply no credible evidence that the Framers of the Fourteenth Amendment sought "to transfer the security and protection of all the civil rights ... from the states to the Federal government. The Slaughter-House Cases, 16 Wall. 36, 77-78, 21 L.Ed 394(1873). The three Reconstruction Amendments undeniably "worked a dramatic change in the balance between congressional and state power, ante, at 720: they forbade state-sanctioned slavery, forbade the state-sanctioned denial of the right to vote, and (until the content of the Equal Protection Clause was substantially applied to the Federal Government through the Due Process Clause of the Fifth Amendment) uniquely forbade States to deny equal protection. The Amendments also specifically empowered the Federal Government to combat discrimination at a time when the breadth of federal power under the

The Amendments

constitution was less apparent than it is today. But nothing in the Amendments themselves, or in our long history of interpreting or applying those momentous charters, suggests that *561 States, exercising their police power, are in any way constitutionally inhibited from working alongside the Federal Government in the fight against discrimination and its effects." (Dissenting Opinion of Richmond v. J.A. Croson Co ruling, Associate Justice Thurgood Marshall, 1989).

When reading this paragraph written by Justice Marshall, makes me think that he would be a strong constitutionalist jurist but, in the end, he thought judicial precedent with his emotions rather than with his intellect. He was an intelligent person of high intelligence but sometimes emotions ran high over his remarkable intelligence. The Civil War Amendments or how Marshall calls them, the Reconstruction Amendments, were indeed to bring an end of racial inequality and discrimination. Also, these amendments were to bring equality for all the races of every single natural-born or naturalized person of this American union.

After these amendments were passed, what southern state legislatures did to discredit the black-American community was uncalled for and unconstitutional while giving a free pass to the white-American community. There is no excuse to what they did but, in the end, the Richmond City Council behaved just like these southern legislators did from 1876 to 1955, they just reversed the racism to the other extreme. In the end, all races are equal under the law, no exceptions.

"The majority today sounds a full-scale retreat from the Court's longstanding solicitude to race-conscious remedial efforts "directed toward deliverance of the century-old promise of equality of economic opportunity." *Fullilove*, 448 U.S., at 463, 100 S. Ct., at 2767. The new and restrictive tests it applies scuttle one city's effort to surmount its discriminatory

II. The Fourteenth Amendment, 1868

past, and imperil those of dozens more localities. I, however, profoundly disagree with the cramped vision of the Equal Protection Clause which the majority offers today and with its application of that vision to Richmond, Virginia's, laughable set-aside plan. The battle against pernicious racial discrimination or its effects is nowhere near won. I must dissent." (Dissenting Opinion of Richmond v. J.A. Croson Co ruling, Associate Justice Thurgood Marshall, 1989).

Word of advice to Justice Thurgood Marshall and Justice Henry Billings Brown, you cannot give merit to one race and take it from the other. Either we are all equal or not equal. Justice Antonin Scalia gave the perfect example in how to battle to end racial discrimination and inequality.

If a state agency has a discriminatory pay scale compensating black employees in all positions at 20% less than their nonblack counterparts, it may assuredly promulgate an order raising the salaries of "all black employees" to eliminate the differential." (Concurrence Opinion of Richmond v. J.A. Croson Co ruling, Associate Justice Antonin Scalia, 1989).

Is Scalia then saying that when the salary of the black-American workers get increased, so will the white-American workers? No. They are now all equal but in this real world, merit triumphs over equality and merit does not see color. A black-American worker may see a salary increase over his white-American co-worker and that person achieved it because of merit of his work and not by the color of his skin. That is most important to our American republic.

"I join Justice MARSHALL's perceptive and incisive opinion revealing great sensitivity toward those who have suffered the pains of economic discrimination in the construction trades for so long. I never thought that I would live to see the day when the City of Richmond, Virginia,

The Amendments

the cradle of the Old Confederacy, sought on its own, within a narrow confine, to lessen the stark impact of persistent discrimination. But Richmond, to its great credit, acted. Yet this Court, the supposed bastion of equality, strikes down Richmond's efforts as though discrimination had never existed or was not demonstrated in this particular litigation. Justice MARSHALL convincingly discloses the fallacy and the shallowness of that approach. History is irrefutable, even through one might in themselves—benefit from the wrongs of past decades. So the Court today, regresses. I am confident, however, that, given time, it one day again will do its best to fulfill the great promises of the Constitution's Preamble and of the guarantees embodied in the Bill of Rights—a fulfillment that would make this Nation very special." (Dissenting Opinion of Richmond v. J.A. Croson Co ruling, Associate Justice Harry Blackmun, 1989).

Why are Justices Harry Blackmun and William Brennan surprised to see the City of Richmond behave in this manner? Let us all remember that this was the capital of the nation that condone slavery and fought to maintain it and expand on it. This city has a dark history of shame and they cannot hide their shortcomings. So, they initiated a plan to show reverse racism for one race of people but not to another is just as unconstitutional as when they were devising their plans to enact the 'separate but equal' plan onto the Commonwealth of Virginia.

Justice Blackmun speaks about the rights and guarantees that the constitution gives to the persons. What about the rights and guarantees to the persons of corporations that are not of minority-descend? Justice Blackmun speaks like Justice Billings Brown. All Americans are equal and are treated to have the same rights and guarantees as anybody else.

So, that being the case, I am in solidarity support of Associate Justice Antonin Scalia's Concurrence Opinion.

II. The Fourteenth Amendment, 1868

Also, in solidarity for the Fourteenth Amendment that all American persons based on race are all equal under the law. The specialty for the enactment of the Fourteenth Amendment is quite clear and the there is no ambiguity in its language. It is to treat all persons of this union of sovereign states with equal treatment under law. The genius of the constitution is that it always can be changed to better the lives of its persons. To not only better them but to preserve their liberties that they gained. This Fourteenth Amendment was to preserve it for all persons, male's, and female's racial equal rights under the law and within their bill of rights.

But now we will get to two subjects in where the Fourteenth Amendment's language has been expanded not by the national Congress but by the courts. Where these two areas have been expanded to expand the role of the national government without legislative and state's consent. The beautiful language of the Fourteenth Amendment meant well, but unfortunately it has been misinterpreted incorrectly. Interpreted incorrectly by once again zealous and special interest individuals from the court and influences with no constitutional backing of any kind. As the high court once interpreted that black individuals were never meant to be persons, denied equal justice under law with a separation ideology. And now, the high court jurists interpreted with the same equality of unconstitutionality the issue of life and marriage.

Not regarding the unfair housing market strategy that plagued this nation for many years. But also, the blatant injustice of several minority citizens and non-citizens living on this union that felt the injustice of not being treated with equality under law. There have been not hundreds, but thousands of innocent people mistreated, violated, burglarized, raped, assaulted, and even murdered. Legendary black

The Amendments

American singer Billie Holliday sang a very controversial but true reality song entitled, "Strange Fruit." This song represented the thousands of those innocent men, women, children black people being murdered across these states and denying their bill of rights and Fourteenth Amendment protections. Then in recent years, people like Leonard Deadwyler, Dominic Bradford, Eula May Love, Rodney King, Freddie Gray, Michael Brown, Trayvon Martin, Geore Floyd, and most recently Memphis individual Tyre Nichols.

These names, some living, some deceased, are the remembrance that all persons, no matter if you are white, or a person of color are fully entitled of their bill of rights and full extent of the due process of the law and never be denied.

Indeed, several state governments have violated their person's bill of rights whether a life, liberty, and marriage issue. These rights are protected under the bill of rights. But this is where the powers of indefinite and numerous powers rely mostly on the individual rights above state rights and a special federal government enforcement. As much as people like to involve themselves in the court procedure. The question defining these issues are better defined in their own state legislature and individual rights, rather than in federal court.

B. Immigration and Citizenship Relations

"Section I. All persons born or naturalized in the United States, and subject to the jurisdiction thereof, are citizens of the United States and of the State wherein they reside."

"nor shall any State deprive any person of life, liberty, or property, without due process of law; nor deny to any person within its jurisdiction the equal protection of the laws."

If the federal government's high court would not have denied the immigration and naturalization enforcement for each individual sovereign state in the 1850s. We would not be having this debate to this day and being manacled by a current, extreme rogue and arrogant federal government executive administration.

But unfortunately, the federal high court forced the states to "cede" these powers to the general government.

"...that it was necessary that many rights of sovereignty which the States then possessed should be ceded to the General Government..." – Roger Taney.

An arrogant quote from an arrogant chief justice of our high court. A quote that even the constitutional framers would be astounded with disgust.

But again, unfortunately with the meddling of the general government in the businesses of the sovereign states

The Amendments

because of various states failed to follow the newly reshaped constitution. We had the federal government come in and expand their powers, appropriate at first, but inappropriate later. The creation of the of the Fourteenth Amendment was an appropriate force of action. That has completely reshaped our republic into a form, still supporting the idea of human and civil rights and liberties, but with a precarious grey area of enforcement.

And with these unprecedented and somewhat unconstitutional actions from the federal government, it increased their control into the naturalization clause. The first cause of actions was targeting Chinese immigrants immigrating into California and the western states. The first congressional act was in 1875, The Page Act that brought discrimination and racism towards the Chinese community. It was not the federal government's act that brought racism and discrimination. As you may recall the 1850 Fugitive Slave Act that indeed brought upon us the civil war against our beloved sovereign states.

The creation of the Fourteenth Amendment was to give equality under law to our persons residing in our republic, within the first federal government and sovereign state to have equal and due process protection of the law. Given the history of the amendment's creation, debate, and passage. Members of the black community, who were once the enslaved community, were being denied equal protection of the laws. This was just after the civil war and hence, I would say, people must read its history as well as the amendment.

I still believe that if the federal government gave us this right of citizenship, non-citizenship for the individual. But the enforcement aspect of this citizenship immigration and naturalization clause still belongs to the states.

II. The Fourteenth Amendment, 1868

Right now, the current, 2025-2029, federal executive branch, ignorant to the federal constitution are trying to disregard and discourage the birthright citizenship clause. As the said amendment clearly states and the court ruling that set the precedent, birthright citizenship is constitutional.

If I read the last sentence of Section I of the said amendment. A state cannot refuse or deny the bill of rights protections of the "person" residing in a state. If a state refuses to comply to protect the "persons" bill of rights. Then it is the role of the federal government under Section V to come in and enforce that protection with appropriate legislation. The Fourteenth does not state a role for the federal government to deny a persons' (person's and non-person's) bill of rights. And the court is not there to re-write the Constitution, that is not their role…it is the role for Congress.

Regarding the most recent and appropriate situation of a person (non-person) abuse by the federal government, Mr. Kilmar Abrego Garcia. Mr. Garcia entered the United States in 2011, via an unorthodox method entry. But if you are a true constitutionalist, federal immigration law remains to be unconstitutional. He married and had a family with an American person, raising his living status into a more legal status in this union. Again, under the jurisdiction of Maryland, he is subject under the protection of the laws and rights within that state or any other state he resides.

Unfortunately, for the federal government and this current executive branch, they have no jurisdiction to enforce any immigration enforcement law. If that state wishes to nullify and refuse to cooperate. You cannot reason with a madman when his gun is in your mouth.

The method of deportation of this individual by the general government has been totally unconstitutional and the high court has even stated it. They even stated that this union's general government must facilitate his re-entry back into the country, it was in unanimous consent.

Mr. Kilmar Abrego Garcia has been returned to the United States to face criminal charges in the sovereign state of Tennessee for trafficking "supposed" undocumented workers. Let the due process system work for our nation and our people residing in our American union of sovereign states. We the people and the States cannot let our executive branches dictate due process. Due Process continues to be a wonderful tool for liberty and will continue to work without the introduction of centralized-federal tyranny.

We have due process, not protective custody in this republic. Our leaders and people should know this!

* * *

The issue of who is allowed in this union to share our rights and liberties have been an ongoing debate. Sometimes it has become a very contradicting and harsh way to debate leading up to violent hate speech and resulting to violent acts. But as the Americans that we are to co-exist. We must put aside all evil sentiment and read the Constitution well to fully interpret what the framers stated, but *ALSO* to what the Fourteenth Amendment framers intended to dictate.

The constitutional issue of immigration and citizenship relations does not speak of Americanism or citizenry. It speaks of individualism and persons. I believe the constitutional framers did not have any clauses relating to nationwide citizenry because they believed in our unique American rules of federalism. This is what many media mainstream political and historical pundits will fail to claim. They never speak of the sovereignty of a state to claim this naturalization right. It is my firm belief that the framers of our Constitution intended to give this enforcement right to the individual

II. The Fourteenth Amendment, 1868

states, not to the central government authority. While the amendment authors were crafting this article, they had the framer's thoughts in mind while having the central governmental authority being an administrative and recognized aspect of the citizenry of the individual.

But somehow along the way, national (radical) and several state legislators decided to blatantly hand the reins of immigration and naturalization enforcement to the federal government. With its first unconstitutional act against the first attack on hard-working immigrants entering our union of sovereign states to make a better life for all.

* * *

It was attack on Chinese female immigrants entering our Pacific-Western states. The Page Act of 1875 restricting just that and ending an open border situation that was allowed even prior to the unfortunate civil war conflict. This immigration enforcement act from the general government introduced itself to an attack on the idea of state sovereignty, but to the principles of federalism. This was not the first central government attack on the liberties and rights on people entering and residing within this American union of sovereign states. When centralized power seizes control, it silences individual liberty and sovereignty.

The General Government of the United States has truly become more arrogant than when it first enacted its first federal immigration statute in 1875.

When this General Government and several state governments create control under the idea of fear...it silences liberty. That is what the General Government has always done in bringing that control by using fear. They used it in 1850, used it in 1875, and have constantly been using it to its current terms of our American republic.

The Amendments

In 1884, when the crisis of our American Indians was in a precarious and dangerous situation. A tribe member of Winnebago, born in the United States, decided to renounce his tribal allegiance, and tried to become a United States citizen. His voter registration application was denied by a very racist and bigoted individual. Any *"PERSON"* born in the jurisdiction of the United States and resides in a state is automatically a citizen. Even this person is entitled to our bill of rights and protections guaranteed by our Bill of Rights and affirmed by the Fourteenth Amendment.

But unfortunately, the high court of the land did not want to affirm this native-born individual his citizenship and bill of rights protections and denied it to him. It was not the Supreme Court that affirmed this person's rights but Congress in 1924 with the support of President Calvin Coolidge. It took forty years for our American Indian brothers and sisters of this union to receive citizenship rights and bill of rights protections.

It was NOT a shame that the high court in 1898 did come to unanimous consent regarding the immigration case of *United States v. Wong Kim Ark*, 1898. The holding of this case was crystal clear as the language of the Fourteenth Amendment.

In asking for the general government to take the commands to enforce the immigration and naturalization clause is not something that I will ever condone. This has opened to a different wavelength of abusive, contradicting, and arrogant form of power.

It clearly stated that:

a) A child born in the United States to alien parents is a person.
b) The phrase "subject to the jurisdiction thereof" should be interpreted "in light of the common law."

II. The Fourteenth Amendment, 1868

This language of this ruling is clear as apparent to the language of the Fourteenth Amendment. Anyone born within the realm of the United States is a natural-born person or naturalized person.

With the phrase of "subject to the jurisdiction thereof", it is also quite clear to the common-sense constitutional mind. These individuals or in the word of the Fourteenth Amendment, "Persons". If they commit a crime, whether federal and/or state charge, these persons will be considered for prosecution and be given full due process of the law.

This country from its founding to its constitutional adoption does not show a caste system and cannot discriminate against anybody regardless of race, color, and sex.

It is quite clear in the language of the Fourteenth Amendment. This amendment has reshaped the republic to the end vile racism and bigotry that was occurring during 1850-1865.

As much as right-wing nationalists despise some of the actions of the Fourteenth Amendment. Much of the work of this amendment has reshaped our republic to a well-more perfect union. We must keep respecting it, keep reshaping it, and always maintaining it for the future of our American union of sovereign states to be preserved.

Never confuse nationalism with patriotism. To be a nationalist implies for central authoritarian control. To be a patriot implies to apply the wisdom of the constitutional framers to shape and reshape our principled document for the good of our federal American union of sovereign states.

The Supreme Court in the later years of the Twentieth century in its infinite constitutional wisdom has affirmed the Fourteenth Amendment on its true meaning and definition.

The Amendments

In 1980, the ruling of *Vance v. Terrazas* gave us, the individuals who has achieved that it cannot be taken away against his will. The intent to give up or taken away needs to be established by itself and cannot be presumed merely because a "person" did something established by law as an action automatically causing his loss of citizenship. But, however, Congress, NOT the executive branch has the power to decide that an intent to give up citizenship may be established by a preponderance of evidence.

"The formal oath [of allegiance to Mexico] adds nothing to the existing foreign citizenship. In addition, that since Congress has provided for a procedure by which one may formally renounce citizenship" before US consular officials, a procedure that all conceded that Terrazas did not use, Terrazas was still a US citizen." (Dissenting opinion of Vance v. Terrazas, 1980 by Associate Justice William Brennan).

Even the Court has stated that the one branch of power to review citizenship status is Congress...not the federal government executive branch. So, the actions of various executive branches that this union has endured included this current one, these actions remain unconstitutional.

The right to travel across this great American union of sovereign states should never be denied or obtained any sense of fear, discrimination, or reprisal to whatever is your status. *Saenz v. Roe*, 1999 held that a California statute to limit new residents' benefits for the first year they live in the state is an unconstitutional discrimination and violation of their right to travel. Every state is sovereign and has their own set of laws, but federal constitutional amendments, supersedes state law. The three legal, constitutional points in where a "person" has a right to travel from one state to another is listed below:

II. The Fourteenth Amendment, 1868

1. The right to enter one state and leave another;
2. The right to be treated as a welcome visitor rather than a hostile stranger;
3. For those who want to become permanent residents, the right to be treated equally to native-born citizens.

(Opinion Brief of Saenz v. Roe, 1999 by Associate Justice John Paul Stevens)

* * *

Even children of non-persons are protected under the Fourteenth Amendment, Section I. *Plyler v. Doe*, 1982. This ruling stated that the denial of public education to students not legally admitted into the country violates the Equal Protection Clause, Court of appeals for the Fifth Circuit affirmed it. And so, did the United States high court.

"When a state provides an education provides an education to some and denies it to others, it immediately and inevitably creates class distinctions of a type fundamentally inconsistent with the purposes of the Equal Protection Clause because of "an uneducated child is denied even the opportunity to achieve." (Concurring Opinion of Plyler v. Doe, Associate Justice Harry Blackmun, 1982).

* * *

From all justices in the national high court with great constitutional conviction. The one that stands out was as the late Associate Justice John Paul Stevens called him, Justice Antonin "Nino" Scalia.

I quite respected Justice Stevens, but as many have passed through the high court, he shares not so quite the constitutional wisdom that was from the framers of our constitution. He shared constitutional legislative wisdom from the bench while Justice Nino Scalia found deep constitutional wisdom from the pens of our framers.

The Amendments

In an immigration case based on refugee status, I stand in human rights principle with the court. In defining refugee status, I believe it is defined by economically, politically, and human rights status to apply as a refugee status. But I stand in constitutional rights principle with Nino Scalia.

"His opinion concurring in the judgment in *INS v. Cardoza-Fonseca* severely criticized my majority opinion for its reliance on legislative history rather than just statutory text and, more importantly, misapplying the rule announced in *Chevron*, which I authored four years earlier." (The Making of a Justice: Reflections on My First 94 Years, Justice Paul Stevens, Little Brown and Company, 2019, p. 228).

The holding of this 1987 immigration case was "To establish eligibility for asylum under Section 208(a) of the Immigration and Nationality Act, an alien must show only a well-founded fear of persecution, which is something less than a 50% probability of being persecuted if he returns to his home country."

In a course of human rights decision, I also believed in Justice Scalia's constitutional rights statement.

"Judges interpret laws rather than reconstruct legislators' intentions. Where the language of those laws is clear, we are not free to replace it with an unenacted legislative intent." (Concurring Opinion of *INS v. Cardoza-Fonseca* by Associate Justice Antonin Scalia, 1987).

"A judge is not here to prove their legislative's intent but rather their constitutional intent. With that constitutional intent, that should motivate enough for the legislator to apply it in their legislative intent." Rest in Peace, Justice Nino Scalia, I will always continue to reflect your constitutional wisdom on your legacy and mine. Thank you.

This Immigration and Nationality Act should never had come into existence. I strongly believe that no federal immigration act should have come into existence. But when the

II. The Fourteenth Amendment, 1868

general government of the United States has taken the reins on the immigration and naturalization clause away from the power of the individual state governments. We must rely on the wisdom of national legislators to always do the right thing, not the popular thing.

* * *

After the terrible event of 9/11, our union of sovereign states went from a secure, semi-tranquil and sometimes dangerous to lose our liberty to a total control of our lives by a ruling fiat and congressional act of fear.

I am here to involve what is required of the federal government in the issues of immigration and citizenship and naturalization. Even after the terrible event of 9/11, there are still rules set within our constitution that makes us a union of laws, not of Trumpism.

We are now entering a wave of federal immigration measures not passed by Congress but passed by a wave of presidential executive decrees. This an abuse of a continuing rogue and arrogant federal government during peace time or war time within our union of sovereign states. We saw it in the various immigration control executive orders and in the opinion and dissent of *Trump v. Hawaii, (2018)* during Trump's arrogant first term. We are seeing under Trump's second, non-consecutive term.

"Under the Immigration and Nationality Act [of 1965], foreign nationals seeking entry into the United States undergo a vetting process to ensure that they satisfy the numerous requirements for admission. The Act also vests the President with authority to restrict the entry of aliens whenever he finds that their entry "would be detrimental to the interests of the United States." 8 U.S.C. Section 1182(f). Relying on that delegation, the President concluded that it was necessary

The Amendments

to impose entry restrictions on nationals of countries that do not share adequate information for an informed entry determination., or that otherwise present national security risks. Presidential Proclamation No. 9645, 82 Fed. Reg. 45161 (2017) (Proclamation)." (Opinion Brief of Donald J. Trump, President of the United States, Et At., Petitioners v. Hawaii by Chief Justice John Roberts, 2018).

"Nor could it, since the President has inherent authority to exclude aliens from the country." (Concurring Brief of Donald J. Trump, President of the United States, Et At., Petitioners v. Hawaii by Associate Justice Clarence Thomas, 2018).

Says who? The Constitution does not grant this elusive and extreme authority by the chief executive of this republic. This is just several plain and ignorant members of Congress that wanted, and someone continues to want to install this power onto the national executive branch without consulting the Constitution.

"In sum, universal injunctions are legally and historically dubious. If the federal courts continue to issue them, this Court is dutybound to adjudicate their authority to do so." (Concurring Brief of Donald J. Trump, President of the United States, Et At., Petitioners v. Hawaii by Associate Justice Clarence Thomas, 2018).

"Our Constitution demands, and our country deserves, a Judiciary willing to hold to coordinate branches to account when they defy our most sacred legal commitments. Because the Court's decision today has failed in that respect, with profound regret, I dissent." (Dissenting Brief of Donald J. Trump, President of the United States, Et At., Petitioners v. Hawaii by Associate Justice Sonia Sotomayor, 2018).

We saw in 2017-2021 the vast disregard of our courts system in where the executive branch made a mockery of our Article III, in where it gives the judiciary branch the power to question these edicts. These universal injunctions are not defined by Article III or defined by the Judiciary Act of 1789 by Congress. It is for Congress, not the Courts to

II. The Fourteenth Amendment, 1868

define them. Also, in where we could not interpret them or let Congress decide to question these themselves. In the end, it is Congress who decides because they control the funding, not the executive or the judiciary branches. In 2017, Congress did not give this authority to the federal executive branch to pursue, arrest, and deport anybody, especially without the due process initiative embedded in our Bill of Rights.

And we continue to see this blatant disregard of the executive branch, during the Biden administration and now under the second, non-consecutive term of the Trump administration.

"On December 8, 2015, Trump justified his proposal during a television interview by noting that President Franklin D. Roosevelt "did the same thing" with respect to the internment of Japanese Americans during World War II." (Dissenting Brief of Donald J. Trump, President of the United States, Et At., Petitioners v. Hawaii by Associate Justice Sonia Sotomayor, 2018).

"What I am doing is no different than FDR."
– Donald J. Trump on Good Morning America, December 8, 2015.

When somebody decides to justify his/her actions by defending the actions of others, especially when those actions are unconstitutional and immoral, it is strictly deplorable and despicable. The basis of Proclamation No. 9645 is truly no different than Executive Order No. 9066. They both contain a sheer level of arrogance toward the rules of federalism. But we can expect nothing from populist demagogues from the FDR administration and the Trump administration. Populist demagogues have no political party affiliation or principle affiliation. They just have tyrannical affiliation.

The Amendments

That is what we are seeing now within this new administration of Donald J. Trump. Again, the second, non-consecutive term of Trump has begun a rampant of policies and orders that not only are blatantly unconstitutional. But these orders are continuing not to be allowed to be challenged by our Article III in our national constitution.

The Spanish Ambassador once asked President Martin van Buren during the Amistad case, in why do you have such judicial independent arrogance from the courts in where the executive cannot govern. And President van Buren quickly and constitutionally responded, "as any true American will tell you, it is the independence of our courts that keeps us free."

It is the independence of our entire American republic union of sovereign states' Constitution that keeps us free from tyrannical orders from central governance and state government governance.

"On January 20, 2025, President Trump issued Executive Order 14,160, protecting the meaning and value of American citizenship. This order reflects the original meaning of the Fourteenth Amendment, which guaranteed citizenship to the children of former slaves, not to illegal aliens or temporary visitors." (Oral Argument of Trump v. CASA, Incorporated, and consolidated cases, by Solicitor General D. John Sauer, 2025).

"Multiple district orders promptly issued nationwide or universal injunctions blocking this order, and a cascade of such universal injunctions followed. Universal injunctions exceed the judicial power granted in Article III, which exists only to address the injury to the complaining party." (Oral Argument of Trump v. CASA, Incorporated, and consolidated cases, by Solicitor General D. John Sauer, 2025).

"And they disrupt the Constitution's careful balancing of the separation of powers." (Oral Argument of Trump v. CASA, Incorporated, and consolidated cases, by Solicitor General D. John Sauer, 2025).

II. The Fourteenth Amendment, 1868

When you have multiple court orders stating that one order is unconstitutional. That should tell you something that there is something wrong with our executive leadership. A person has every right to bring in a complaint against the government, federal and state, if there is an injustice. The powers are carefully separated from one another and separated within themselves.

There is no disruption needed if any executive government entity does not violate the constitution principle bill of rights of its persons. That is exactly my definition of separation of powers among this republic. The esteemed Solicitor General also forgot the explanation of 'checks and balances' among the separation of powers.

Each power is independent from one another and independent from themselves, but the power of checks and balances rests on each other to maintain the peace and unity.

"Here, there's a discrete identified group on one issue: Does citizenship mean are you born in the territory of the United States, or does it mean are you loyal to someone else, which is your claim, or are your parents loyal to someone else?" (Oral Argument of Trump v. CASA, Incorporated, and consolidated cases, Question by Associate Justice Sonia Sotomayor, 2025).

An important issue regarding the Bill of Rights and affirmation of the Fourteenth Amendment is that 'All persons residing within this union and territories are equal under law.' There is no sense of privilege under law, in this union and the Constitution is quite clear in its language.

"No, we don't, because the argument here is that the president is violating an established - - not just one but, by my count four established Supreme Court precedents. We have the *Wong Ark* case, where we said fealty to a foreign sovereign doesn't defeat your entitlement to citizenship as a child. We have another case where we said that even if your parents are here illegally, if you're born here, you're a citizen." (Oral Argument of Trump v. CASA, Incorporated, and consolidated cases, Question by Associate Justice Sonia Sotomayor, 2025).

"In appropriate cases, courts have certified class actions on an emergency basis. We found at least four cases in recent years where that was done. But, more fundamentally, we profoundly disagree with the characterization of the merits. This is now fully briefed in the Ninth Circuit in Case Number 25-807, where we describe how that characterization of the holding of *Wong Kim Ark* and other decisions is profoundly incorrect." (Oral Argument of Trump v. CASA, Incorporated, and consolidated cases, by Solicitor General D. John Sauer, 2025).

How would you conclude that the *Wong Kim Ark* ruling was constitutionally incorrect? Either this administration's is quite the illiterate or deep a bigoted and racist administration in modern American political history. It is quite stated in its first sentence of Section I of the amendment. *'All persons born or naturalized in the United States, and subject to the jurisdiction thereof, are citizens of the United States and of the State, wherein they reside'*.

The language is so clear, even a third-grade student would understand this type of wording in our Constitution. Now the ruling of *Trump v. Hawaii*, 2018 and this current case is an invasion, not of individual state sovereignty. But these cases are a serious violation of individual right sovereignty. It is not a violation of citizenship or non-citizenship. It is a violation of what is described in our Fourteenth Amendment and the language as clear as apparent as its amendment authors wrote it and has been quite interpreted that way for all people within our American union.

"- - so, when a new president orders that because there's so much gun violence going on in the country and he comes in and he says, I have the right to take away the guns from

II. The Fourteenth Amendment, 1868

everyone, then people - - and he sends out the military to seize everyone's guns - - we and the courts have to sit back and wait until every named plaintiff gets - - or every plaintiff whose gun is taken comes into court?" (Oral Argument of Trump v. CASA, Incorporated, and consolidated cases, Question by Associate Justice Sonia Sotomayor, 2025).

I rarely agree with Associate Justice Sonia Sotomayor on practically everything, but in defining the Fourteenth Amendment and the power of Article III against an intrusive federal executive branch. I must side with Justice Sotomayor and not with tyranny.

Immigration and citizenship violation questions, gun violation questions are all to proceed in lower and high court proceedings and constitutionally justified.

"Okay. So - - but it sounds to me like you accept a *Cooper versus Aaron* kind of situation for the Supreme Court, but not for, say, the Second Circuit? In other words, you would respect the opinions and the judgments of the Supreme Court, and you're saying you would respect the judgment but not necessarily the opinion of a lower court." (Oral Argument of Trump v. CASA, Incorporated, and consolidated cases, Question by Associate Justice Amy Coney Barrett, 2025).

"And, again, and I think in the vast majority of instances our practice has been to respect the opinions as well, in - - in the circuits as well, but my understanding that has not been categorical practice in the way respect for the precedence and in judgments that the Supreme Court has been." (Oral Argument of Trump v. CASA, Incorporated, and consolidated cases, by Solicitor General D. John Sauer, 2025).

"So you're not hedging at all with respect to the precedent of this Court?" (Oral Argument of Trump v. CASA, Incorporated, and consolidated cases, Question by Associate Justice Amy Coney Barrett, 2025).

The Amendments

"That is correct." (Oral Argument of Trump v. CASA, Incorporated, and consolidated cases, by Solicitor General D. John Sauer, 2025).

A lower court ruling must be obeyed until the appeals process is complete and a final judgment has been heard and set. That is the beauty of Article III to protect the persons rights under the Constitution.

One thing that we must understand about our sacred Constitution is that our government, federal and state are not here to violate our rights but protect our rights from any injustice.

The question regarding this present case or the ruling decision of *Trump v. Hawaii* is not of an overstepped lower court boundary. The question, in my constitutional opinion is if the federal executive branch has indeed overstepped their boundaries and not only initiated deportation policies, but initiated deportation policies without due process. I quote from the father and writer of the Constitution, James Madison, "A power nowhere delegated to the federal government," 1798.

From all the Supreme Court justices appointed by the President Trump. I find Justice Amy C. Barrett to be more in line with its constitutional founding and meaning. Justice Barrett relies more in inscribing the constitution's values without getting emotional unlike other members of the high court.

As we waited for the Supreme Court's interpretation on these lower court injunctions for the issue of deportations on the issue of the Fourteenth Amendment and the constitutional birthright citizenship issue. Whether how the high court leans from one side or the other side, remember that the Constitution, as it is currently written that 'All Persons, (citizens and non-citizens) are equal under law'.

* * *

II. The Fourteenth Amendment, 1868

President Donald J. Trump's Executive Order #14160: Protecting the Meaning and Value of American Citizenship

I question this unconstitutional federal Executive Order. The national government knows truly little of values and knows a great deal of protective custody… especially this administration.

"The Executive Order identifies circumstances in which a person born in the United States is not "subject to the jurisdiction thereof" and is thus not recognized as an American citizen." (Opinion of the Court of Trump v. CASA, Inc., by Associate Justice Amy Coney Barrett, 2025).

The national government, whether the executive, Congress, or Supreme Court are now in the business of expanding the realm of the federal government. Unfortunately, it is Congress to blame for giving this power of naturalization to the executive branch, and not to the sovereign states to enforce. Thank you, Roger Taney.

As the American republic keeps turning on and on more into a dependent nation. The general government keeps increasing in unconstitutional and unprecedented enforcement power under the Naturalization clause. The Supreme Court gave its ruling on June 27, 2025 on a very trivial and unorthodox fashion towards the definition of the rules of federalism.

Even with a six to three majority decision, President Trump still claims that the high court has overruled the Citizenship clause of the Fourteenth Amendment. He was making the claim that the Citizenship clause was for the "babies of slaves" and not to "people who come in and want to abuse the system."

The Amendments

"Babies of slaves?!" I hate to break it to the president and his fanatical movement of MAGA. But there were no slaves when the Fourteenth Amendment was adopted. The Fourteenth was adopted in 1868. The abolition of slavery occurred in 1865 with the Thirteenth Amendment's adoption. I sure hope, President Trump does not wish to find a way to be rid of this amendment.

As far as, denying people on the baseless claim that they come in to abuse the system, natural-born, naturalized citizens, permanent residents from all walks of life abuse the system to gain some sort of dependency from the federal government or from their state government.

But the high court has not, or I do not believe they will rule on the constitutionality of the Citizenship clause of the Fourteenth. This ruling was merely based on the constitutionality of universal injunctions. If so, if they violate Article III or the defined law of the Judiciary Act of 1789.

The main objective of this case was to reduce the power of the federal government's executive branch on executive orders by way of the courts.

I do not question the legality of the courts, I believe we need the courts to offer legality and accountability to the other branches of government, including the judiciary. But there are certain areas of government that some branches should not intercede, and it should be shared and conducted within the same decorum of the idea of separation of powers.

In order to examine the type of lower court objection and in other words, injunction. We must examine what the Judiciary Act of 1789 entails and if it needs to be examined by the courts or by Congress. But before we examine this act, let us examine if the federal government has the right to enforce this naturalization clause and take no regard to let the states enforce it on their own accord.

II. The Fourteenth Amendment, 1868

"The States maintain that the District Court made the right call. See Opposition to Application in No. 24A886 (New Jersey), at 31-39. As the States see it, their harms—financial injuries and the administrative burdens flowing from citizen-dependent benefits programs—cannot be remedied without a blanket ban on the enforcement of the Executive Order." (Opinion of the Court of Trump v. CASA, Inc., by Associate Justice Amy Coney Barrett, 2025).

New Jersey opposed this injunction application... what can we expect from the Garden State. They milk the federal government for funds to be more dependent than any southern state.

"The Government—unsurprisingly—sees matters differently. It retorts that even if the injunction is designed to benefit only the States, it is "more burdensome than necessary to redress their asserted harms." (Opinion of the Court of Trump v. CASA, Inc., by Associate Justice Amy Coney Barrett, 2025).

The era of American dependency continues within our nation. I do not care what or how the federal government sees it differently or similar. We the sovereign States are not beholden to the national government or dependent off it.

Unfortunately, the sovereign states had lost sovereignty retainment way before 1913. There were several states, predominately in the south, seeking dependency from the national government. But 1913 sealed the fate of the state sovereign doctrine with the adoption of the two most unprincipled amendments to enter into the Constitution.

So, for Justice Barrett to call it "citizen-benefited" programs is beyond hypocritical. Please call it as it rightfully should, "sanctioned-robbery programs." Sanctioned-robbery programs orchestrated by the unprincipled Sixteenth Amendment.

The Amendments

At least Justice Barrett recognizes the "era of dependency" that has now plagued our republic. But unfortunately, the court cannot remedy anything to alleviate from this dependency, because it is Congress's job to alleviate this remedy. But to suggest that the state governments need the federal government rather than the other way around is absolute arrogance. This Constitution was made by the sovereign states, not by the federal government.

This case's opinion's entails as follows, "Universal injunctions likely exceed the equitable authority that Congress has given to federal courts. The Court grants the Government's applications for partial stay of the injunctions entered below, but only to the extent that the injunctions are broader than necessary to provide complete relief to each plaintiff with standing to sue." (Opinion of the Court of Trump v. CASA, Inc., by Associate Justice Amy Coney Barrett, 2025).

Nowhere in this holding of this case does the majority of the justices deny the existence or even overrule the Citizenship clause of the Fourteenth Amendment. The Court is again issuing the dangers of what authority a lower court has the authority as defined by the Judiciary Act of 1789. If an individual wishes to explore a better definition of "universal injunction", then propose it to your Member of the national House of Representatives to redefine the law.

"The question whether Congress has granted federal courts the authority to universally enjoin the enforcement of an executive or legislative policy plainly warrants our review, as Members of this Court have repeatedly emphasized." (Opinion of the Court of Trump v. CASA, Inc., by Associate Justice Amy Coney Barrett, 2025).

The American individual so desperately need to read well, not only the Constitution, but the congressional acts but more importantly the constitutional opinions of the high court.

II. The Fourteenth Amendment, 1868

"If [universal injunctions'] popularity continues, this Court must address their legality." (Concurring Opinion of the Court of Trump v. Hawaii, by Associate Justice Clarence Thomas, 2018).

If [universal injunctions'] popularity continues, it is Congress to address their legality, not the courts.

This is not the first time in where the high court has explained the role of the lower court's role regarding issuing "universal injunctions." But maybe, I am the only one that understands the role of the federal government branches and how they are supposed to function to exist.

In Article III of the Constitution speaks of the roles and powers of the judiciary branch. But there is indeed no mention of universal injunction by a lower, or appellate courts. It is not the job of the courts to rewrite a law or amend the Constitution. That we much know of the proper functions of the judiciary.

The lack of education among our American individuals is quite astounding in where they wish to bypass one branch of government and give it to another. The sense of the education of the American individual stands from all sides in the political parties and movements.

It is not very becoming of the Protectors of the Constitution to bicker and attack one another. Argue, yes, we are all entitled to our First Amendment Free Speech clause. But to attack each other because of their differences of opinions is beyond for any American, especially our high court jurists. They are there to maintain the follow the Constitution. As well as maintain the integrity of the highest court of the land. As much as many disagreed with Justice Harlan's dissent on *Plessy v. Ferguson*, 1896. The author of the opinion of the court Justice Brown did not attack his fellow jurist.

The Amendments

"If so, her position goes far beyond the mainstream defense of universal injunctions." (Opinion of the Court of Trump v. CASA, Inc., by Associate Justice Amy Coney Barrett, 2025).

"We will not dwell on JUSTICE JACKSON's argument, which is at odds with more than two centuries' worth of precedent, not to mention the Constitution itself. We observe only this: JUSTICE JACKSON decries an imperial Executive while embracing an imperial Judiciary." (Opinion of the Court of Trump v. CASA, Inc., by Associate Justice Amy Coney Barrett, 2025).

I hate to burst the bubble of the majority opinion of the Court and the dissenting opinions of the court regarding this case. In this republic, there is nothing remotely close to anything imperial. The Constitution forbids it, while ignorance is allowing it.

For Justice Jackson and Justice Barrett to even entertain this thought is beyond reprehensible.

"No one disputes that the Executive has a duty to follow the law." (Opinion of the Court of Trump v. CASA, Inc., by Associate Justice Amy Coney Barrett, 2025).

"[E]veryone, from the President on down, is bound by law." *Ibid*. That goes for judges too." (Opinion of the Court of Trump v. CASA, Inc., by Associate Justice Amy Coney Barrett, 2025).

Actually, nobody should dispute that the Executive has a duty to follow the Constitution. Laws get amended or repealed but the Constitution remains. Everyone, from the president on down, is bound by the Constitution and nothing more. We swear an oath to uphold, protect, defend, and maintain the Constitution, not simple laws that are meant to expire or repeal.

"Tragically, the majority also shuns this prescient warning: Even if "[s]uch institutions may be destined to pass away," "it is the duty of the Court to be last, not first, to give them

II. The Fourteenth Amendment, 1868

up." (Dissenting Opinion of the Court of Trump v. CASA, Inc., by Associate Justice Ketanji Brown Jackson, 2025).

Disappointedly, the entire Court has shunned the very idea of American constitutional federalism. Neither the opinion of this Court or the dissenting ones know the very meaning of American constitutionalism. "it is the utmost duty of the Court to fully interpret the Constitution and its defining laws to the letter of its wordings. And any flaws of that interpretation, the Court must be compelled to hand their opinion to the national Congress or to the individual state government legislature for revision of that law to be aligned with the national Constitution.

I thought to believe the high court was going to speak about the Citizenship clause of the Fourteenth Amendment. But they at last did not and am quite happy of that notion. They only spoke of the unnecessary and proper power of lower court universal injunctions. Lower court decisions can pass injunctions as they pertain to their jurisdiction. To go past their jurisdiction to pursue a special interest agenda, and against the national government is not the American federalism way.

The movement of MAGA believes in an obscure and quite extreme of "America First" policies for our republic. I do believe in America first, but in the words of our beloved thirtieth president of our American republic of sovereign states, Calvin Coolidge.

"The generally expressed desire of "America first" cannot be criticized. It is a perfectly correct aspiration for our people to cherish. But the problem which we have to solve is how to make America first. It cannot be done by the cultivation of national bigotry, arrogance, or selfishness. Hatreds, jealousies, and suspicions will not be productive of any benefits in this direction. Because there are other peoples whose ways are not our ways, and whose thoughts are not our thoughts,

The Amendments

we are not warranted in drawing the conclusion that they are adding nothing to the sum of civilization." (Foundations of the Republic, Toleration and Liberalism, Calvin Coolidge, University of the Press of the Pacific, Honolulu, Hawaii, p. 299-300).

"We do not need to be too loud in the assertion of our own righteousness." (Foundations of the Republic, Toleration and Liberalism, Calvin Coolidge, University of the Press of the Pacific, Honolulu, Hawaii, p. 300).

I think in my unbiased constitutional opinion in how to adopt "America First" policies are to be constitutionally responsible. We need to be constitutionally tolerant and put aside all personal resentments and concentrate within the law and the constitution.

If we show any intolerant and hatred ways among our people of this union, we not deserved to be called part of these American union of sovereign states. That is not our American way of life. Yes, we have had past turbulent times within our history, but as all nations need to heal...so those ours.

Right now, the America First movement policy is filled with everything against Coolidge is describing his own policy. This is not the policy for our American union.

"Hatreds, jealousies, and suspicions will not be productive or beneficial to the sanity retainment of our republic's continuing reshaping document." Lawful, care, and justice are the productive benefits in the direction of America First. This is why no wonder who the president of is today, Calvin Coolidge will always be my president of these American union sovereign states.

I have never been in favor of the federal executive branch exceeding the unlawful enforcement of the Naturalization clause and now by possibly restricting the Citizenship clause of the Fourteenth. While I also oppose for universal injunctions, unless defined by Congress. I dissent on actual constitutional grounds on *Trump v. CASA, Inc.*, 2025.

C. Section III Enforcement

We come to an important aspect in discussing the Fourteenth Amendment. This issue has been quite disregarded and underrated within our Fourteenth Amendment's language. This section brought safety and security against individuals trying to overthrow our institutions, federal and state. Our republic was made into a union of sovereign states. Which is interpreted as I see it, that when a state enters this constitutional compact, we must abide and respect the enumerated federal acts as well as respect our sovereign states' sovereignty. To make this nation into a more perfect union, a more perfect union of sovereign states, we must respect it and abide to all in accordance with the Constitution.

> Section III. No person shall be a Senator or Representative in Congress, or elector of President and Vice President, or hold any office, civil or military, under the United States, or under any State, who having previously taken an oath, as a member of Congress, or as an officer of the United States, or as an executive or judicial officer of any State, to support the Constitution of the United States, shall have engaged in insurrection or rebellion against the same, or given aid or comfort to the enemies

The Amendments

thereof. But Congress, may by a vote of two-thirds of each House, remove such disability.

After the unfortunate civil war and the patriotization of former confederate rebels back into our American society. Several radical republicans wanted to keep punishing the South, especially after the assassination of President Lincoln. After the trials of Mary Suratt and other confederate rebel insurrectionists, the national Congress needed to secure our national and state institutions from treasonous acts.

Also, many former confederate rebels that re-entered the political scene in various southern states were being a nuisance and denying the newly freed people, their basic rights and keeping them in the fields. Even though slavery was abolished with the Thirteenth Amendment, various former rebellious states were enacting Apprenticeship laws to keep these individuals back in the fields. The national Congress then gave power to the executive to enact martial law in those areas and so began the ill-tempered version of Reconstruction.

But the national Congress knew that they cannot punish the entire south for just a few individuals. So, there was a valid reason to add Section III of the Fourteenth Amendment to maintain tranquility and peace among our American union of sovereign states.

Let us remember that even though the civil war ended the vile form of forced labor production known as slavery, the continuation of our American union of sovereign states remained intact. Just because our nation added new amendments to the constitution, let us not forget that the existing clauses still pertaining to the state sovereign doctrine, alive and well and are still there to function and exist.

"A state cannot exclude any candidate for federal office from the ballot on account of Section 3, and any state that

II. The Fourteenth Amendment, 1868

does so is violating the holding of Term Limits by altering the Constitution's qualifications for federal office." (Donald J. Trump v. Norma Anderson, 2024, Oral Argument of Jonathan F. Mitchell, Petitioner).

In bringing up the Fourteenth Amendment, Section Three, it is not really a grey area in where a state can ban a candidate from running or holding office. The Fourteenth Amendment is not an amendment for the States. It was made for the protection of the national government and a national protection of the American integrity. Where copy is missing from this statement that a true constitutionalist can see, and a true constitutionalist are rare during these fragile republic times. Is that it is Article II, Section I, Clause II gives "a" State, the right to act in such a manner to regulate elections. This is a manner in states regulate their elections, to protect the safety of its persons.

"A state can exclude any candidate for any office from their ballot on account of Article II, not Section III of the Fourteenth."

Constitution 101: There is a difference between the electoral clauses and Section III. The electoral clauses grant the states full right to bar any candidate from running for office. While Section III grants the Congress to bar any individual from holding office in account that person was involved in an insurrection or rebellion. But we are discussing in this book this newly added federal power that reshaped our republic.

The Fourteenth Amendment reshaped the republic to create a heart for humanity and rights for all Americans based on race and color. It reshaped under a new form of federal government enforcement power. But the states still were able to maintain their sovereignty.

A case presented to bring forth a challenge on Section III of the Fourteenth was a Virginia case entitled "The Griffin case."

The Griffin court case was a case during a time of American history that was darker than the period of

The Amendments

Antebellum. This period was known as the "Black Code era" of the American south. After the Confederate States of America was dissolved, and many southerners did not want to abide to the new Thirteenth Amendment. So, they installed suppressive laws against the newly freed Black American individuals known as "Apprenticeship Laws." A freed black man by the name of Caesar Griffin was convicted of an alleged attempted murder charge in rural Virginia in the late 1860's. The judge, Hugh W. Sheffey, presiding in the case, before he was a judge, was the Speaker to the Virginia General Assembly during the civil war in the Confederate States of America.

The convicted man then sued the judge because his ruling should have been overturned because the judge himself would have been considered an insurrectionist as directed under the Fourteenth Amendment. As the judge was a former confederate official that served in one of the state legislatures of the former Confederate States of America. He would be indeed considered as an insurrectionist but for some reason the Chief Justice of the high court acting as the appellate judge during this trial did not agree with Mr. Caesar Griffin.

Yes, this judge would be considered an insurrectionist given that he disavowed the federal constitution and to boot swore an allegiance to another nation. But as the war ended and States were being re-admitted into the union. Many of these ex-confederates returned to their homes and occupations once again.

This case regrettably was a state case and as we know that any challenge made under the Fourteenth Amendment is to be enforced at the federal level, Congress. This lower state argument had no precedent to invoke a Fourteenth Amendment challenge. Congress does, but also regrettably that the membership of fellow congressmen were Republicans

II. The Fourteenth Amendment, 1868

that wanted to appease to both the newly freed black men and women but also to the repatriated former confederate rebels coming back into the union. Congress was not going to remove this confederate judge from the bench being a state issue. If this judge was a federally appointed individual, then the removal would have taken place.

The post-Civil War Courts, or as I like to call it, "The Reconstructive Courts", took it upon themselves to rewrite the Constitution to a newer version of antebellum. Quite frankly, I would never quote anything from the first reconstructive (Chase) court. Maybe, one case, deciding that States have no power to secede, *Texas v. White*, 1869. As my readers and followers know by now is that I am not a secessionist. I do not believe and agree, sovereign States have that power. Once a State enters this constitutional compact, it is their sovereign duty of that State to find ways to maintain and obey the Constitution, both federal and their State. I am a nullificationist and believe in the power of the states' authority over the central power to be able to maintain that sovereignty and independence.

To hear a lawyer quote and agree with Chief Justice Samuel Chase on a ruling that granted protection to an insurrectionist, especially one that never took the oath of allegiance is very alarming and disheartening. I can see why the high court never heard this case because in the end, it was the right decision. In the end, because if we know how the high court would act, they will act the wrong way and the unconstitutional way.

Alexander Stephens, a controversial figure in the war between the states, and former vice-president of the Confederate States of America.

After the state of Georgia was accepted back into the union in mid-1865. Stephens was appointed by the Georgia

The Amendments

state legislature to be their national senator delegate. But the national Senate refused to seat him due to his actions during the civil war. Prior to the Fourteenth's adoption, the actions of the national Senate against Stephens would be considered unconstitutional. If Section III was there prior to 1865, then the national Congress has the absolute authority to bar him from holding office. But the Fourteenth was passed, signed, and ratified after Alexander Stephens was elected to the national Senate to represent his state in Georgia.

You may regard Mr. Alexander Stephens with the utmost disrespect and disgust, and that is quite acceptable in the court of public opinion. But in the court of constitutional law, prior to 1868, we must respect the Constitution and his right to represent his state in the national Congress.

He was appointed to represent Georgia's eighth congressional district. He took that seat in 1873, as the winner of that election, Ambrose R. Wright died before taking the oath of office. The US House of Representatives refuse to seat him and therefore Congress created the Joint Committee on Reconstruction. Again, not in the court of public opinion but in the court in constitutional law is where we must place the crimes and misdemeanors of Mr. Alexander Stephens. After 1868, Congress did that have the explicit authority to bar Stephens and people like Alexander Stephens.

Even after the Fourteenth Amendment was adopted, the vast of constitutional ignorance that was in the realm of the national government remained just as sufficient as in 2024. Stephens did serve multiple terms in the national house of representatives while being a recognized insurrectionist and rebel.

Did the Fourteenth reshape the republic? Because I see the same level of ignorance as prior of its adoption.

1873: If Congress failed to bar Alexander Stephens from holding "federal" office with enough evidence of his treachery

II. The Fourteenth Amendment, 1868

under the authorization of Section III. Then I see no chance in them adopting a similar measure against Donald J. Trump.

The high-level government officials of the now dissolved Confederate States of America were either pardoned or exonerated and entered once again American society. And yet, the current national government officials failed to reign in some justice against these treasonous individuals that broke their constitutional oath, and they should have never entered American society but should have entered prison society.

Now we enter the dilemma of at present individuals that were involved and featured on January 6, 2021. Some constitutional scholars, from both sides of the political party spectrum would have divisive opinions on that day.

Despite in how you view your opinion on Mr. Donald J. Trump. It is just in the realm of public opinion. The opinion court of constitutional law is the only one that must be heard, justified, and enforced.

"Well, why would that be an important - - why would that be permissible? Because Section 3 refers to the holding of office, not running for office. And so, if a state or Congress were to go further and say that you can't run for office, you can't compete in a primary you must have been free from this disqualification at an earlier point in time than Section 3 specifies." (Oral Arguments of Donald J. Trump v. Norma Anderson, 2024, Associate Justice Samuel Alito).

Section III of the Fourteenth Amendment clearly states that the national Congress would bar anyone from holding office, not of running for office. The states do not have this claim under the Fourteenth Amendment power.

"No doubt, States have significant "authority over presidential electors" and, in turn Presidential elections." (Concurring Opinion on Trump v. Anderson by Associate Justices Sonia Sotomayor, Elena Kagan, and Ketanji Jackson, 2024).

The Amendments

"The Reconstruction Amendments "were specifically designed as an expansion of federal power and an intrusion on state sovereignty." (Concurring Opinion on Trump v. Anderson by Associate Justices Sonia Sotomayor, Elena Kagan, and Ketanji Jackson, 2024).

The states have the clear authority on electoral governance under the electoral clauses to bar anybody from running in their elections. While the federal government has a clear authority to bar anybody in holding federal office due to being involved in rebellious and insurrectionist activity under Section III.

The three liberal justices clearly have in mind a good, sharp boundary line to what is federal and state power, but there are quite wrong in using the word "intrusion." The (civil war) Amendments were added to the constitution to indeed the lawful presence of the national government while maintaining the idea of state sovereignty that all persons in all states are treated with equality. It is only intrusive if the states disobey the Fourteenth's language of the law. But regarding Section III and who has the enforcement authority...it is the national Congress of the federal government.

The Fourteenth Amendment brought some cloud in constitutional judgment in some American's mind that forgot the true meaning of the Constitution. To bring an electoral case of a sovereign state to use the Fourteenth Amendment as a source of authority is just as flimsy as bringing up case on abortion or same-sex marriage. If people would have just read the Constitution from the Bill of Rights, to the electoral clauses to Amendment Fourteen. Then Section III would have been rightly and aptly decided and Donald J. Trump would have been rightly justified to be kept off on various states' ballots.

* * *

II. The Fourteenth Amendment, 1868

My final thought on the Fourteenth Amendment regarding racial relations; immigration and citizenship relations, and Section III enforcement. It is a fair and good added addition to our Constitution. But it has been clouded with unfair and biased opinions from challenges not vested within the realm of the Fourteenth amendment. The main principle idea of this amendment is to show to the world that this rightful American union of sovereign states can still co-exist from its constitutional adoption in 1787 to the present. It must put aside all ancient prejudice and treat all persons and non-persons regardless of race, or color, alike to the full equality under law precedence.

The motto for the Fourteenth must always be "All Equal Under Law," by race or color, not by "privileged for some, and deny it to all."

* * *

Any kind of marital relationship, relationship, life, or identity issues does not constitute for any government entity to define it and regulate it. In my constitutional opinion, these issues are not to be reshaped under the Fourteenth Amendment, but under a very sacred and underrated bill of right amendment.

Can you guess which one it is? It is the
Ninth Amendment

"The enumeration in the Constitution, of certain rights, shall not be construed to deny or disparage others retained by the people."

The Ninth Amendment, Bill of Rights of our Constitution

D. Marriage Relations

Marriage has been one of a controlling legal fight within our republic. Whether the national government or the several state governments want to control the marriage stature of our persons. "Control" has been the true enemy of a functioning representative republic.

And this is not the primary functions for the national government or state governments to control the marital lifestyle of their persons. The days before the constitutional 1787 inception, the government of the colonies were controlling the marital lifestyle. Up in New England, the several British colonial governments had marital controlling decrees that even led up to cruel and unusual punishments towards the female persons.

Up until the after the civil war, various southern states were on the verge to control the marital lifestyle of all marriages, including interracial marriages. The Commonwealth of Virginia General Assembly established the 1924 Racial Integrity Act. This unfortunate act reinforced the laws for segregation among the commonwealth's persons. This act gave legitimacy to life-threatening cases in Virginia, (see Part E. Life Relations section Page 156, *Buck v. Bell* 1927). A complete violation not of the Fourteenth but on all of Ms. Buck's bill of rights.

II. The Fourteenth Amendment, 1868

It is quite excruciating that politicians and individuals forget certain aspects of the constitution to please their special interest fanatical and extremist privileged needs. The constitution has no fanatical or extremist point of views, only a strict constitutional point of view. The Constitution holds no privilege under law but equality under law and under the new Fourteenth Amendment statute based on racial relations of all our citizens and non-citizens.

As I stated earlier, the national government and several state governments wanted to control the marriage lifestyle and way of life for our fellow American persons. The case that went down for not only being an invasion of privacy, but an invasion of marriage inequality. It was the 1967 high court decision of *Loving v. Virginia.*

Richard Loving and Mildred Loving Jeter, were indeed an interracial, not the first in our American union history, but the first to show precedence of their constitutional violations of their bill of rights and affirmed by the Fourteenth Amendment.

According to Virginia law, set in the 1924 Racial Integrity Act in which the high court affirmed its constitutionality and not affected by the Fourteenth Amendment. But as we all know this ruling was completely erroneous to our rules of federalism.

The marriage of the Loving couple was considered not valid under various southern states. Not only this couple, were indeed an interracial couple, and yet it fits a perfect precedence challenge under a Fourteenth Amendment violation, as well as also a violation of their due process rights. If the petitioners in the *Obergefell v. Hodges* case were an interracial, and same sex couple and their due process had been violated as it was to the Loving married couple…I would find more constitutional precedence and lawful understanding in their case. But they were a white race, same sex couple. That does not fit the constitutional narrative under the Fourteenth Amendment.

"We have rejected the proposition that the debates in the Thirty-ninth Congress or in the state legislatures which ratified the Fourteenth Amendment supported the theory advanced by [Virginia], that the requirement of equal protection of the laws is satisfied by penal laws defining offenses based on racial classifications as so long as white and Negro participants in the office were similarly punished." (Majority Opinion of Loving v. Virginia, Chief Justice Earl Warren, 1967).

"[Virginia] finds support for its "equal application" theory in the decision of the Court in *Pace v. Alabama*... However, as recently as the 1964 Term, in rejecting the reasoning of that case, we stated "*Pace* represents a limited view of the Equal Protection Clause which has not withstood analysis in the subsequent decisions of the Court." (Majority Opinion of Loving v. Virginia, Chief Justice Earl Warren, 1967).

It is interesting that there were two cases prior to Loving in where the anti-miscegenation laws of the states of Alabama and Florida were upheld by the high court. Both cases, the male was a person of color while the woman was white. In the case of Loving, the male was a white person while the woman was of color. And yet, the high court ruled in favor of the unconstitutional state anti-miscegenation laws.

As you can see, the high court has denied the rights of an individual black man but not the rights of a white woman. Tell it again to the federal government and its high court to create divisions and inequality among the race of persons of this union.

"These statutes also deprive the Lovings of liberty without due process of law in violation of the Due Process of the Fourteenth Amendment. The freedom to marry has long

II. The Fourteenth Amendment, 1868

been recognized as one of the vital personal rights essential to the orderly pursuit of happiness by free men. Marriage is one of the "basic civil rights of man," fundamental to our very existence and survival. To deny this fundamental freedom on so unsupportable a basis as the racial classifications embodied in these statutes, classifications so directly subversive of the principle of equality at the heart of the Fourteenth Amendment, is surely to deprive all the State's persons of liberty without due process of law." (Majority Opinion of Loving v. Virginia, Chief Justice Earl Warren, 1967).

Marriage and adult consensual relationships are indeed one of the basic guaranteed protected rights, and liberties for all American persons. In the cases of *Pace, McLaughlin,* and *Loving,* these cases were in violation of the Fourteenth Amendment. Because they were involved within the race of the American person and their due process rights. The state governments have no right to deny any marriage or consensual relationship of any American adult person regardless of race. But do not confuse the violations of the Fourteenth Amendment rights based on our history and lawful language of the many cases that followed *Loving.* The state governments have no right to deny any marriage or consensual relationship of any American adult person regardless of sex, sexual orientation based on our ninth amendment challenge, not a Fourteenth Amendment challenge. I do believe the high court and the several state governments have indeed gotten it wrong.

* * *

The inequality of marriage and the fight for the definition of marriage and the livelihood has always been a fight with this union. What scares me the most is that the idea of liberty in the privacy of a home has been discouraged by several sovereign states and sometimes affirmed by a federal

The Amendments

high court. I would say that the definition of marriage and the privacy of the American person's home is guaranteed in the bill of rights and affirmed by the individual's Ninth Amendment. There is a reason the right of the individual is before the right of the state, the ninth is before the tenth. But the one difference is that the Fourteenth regards to the race and color of the person to be treated equally under law. It does not say anything about sex, sexual orientation, and gender identity.

In 1984, the high court decided to uphold a Georgia state statute that punished sodomy and the private interaction of two consenting same-sex adults. Writing for the majority was Justice Byron White, a justice appointed by President John F. Kennedy.

"The issue presented is whether the federal Constitution confers a fundamental right upon homosexuals to engage in sodomy and hence invalidates the laws of the many states that still make such conduct illegal and have done so for a very long time. The case also calls for some judgment about the limits of the Supreme Court's role in carrying out its constitutional mandate." (Opinion of Bowers v. Hardwick, Associate Justice Byron White, 1984).

I am trying to evaluate the once oldest-living Associate Justice to the high court of the land, the late John Paul Stevens of Chicago, Illinois. Justice Stevens, being once the most senior member of the court, had seen plenty of cases affecting our people of this great American union of sovereign states. I will examine Stevens' concurring opinion of the 2003 same sex consensual relations case, and his dissent of the one in 1986.

"Our prior cases make two propositions abundantly clear. First, the fact that the governing majority in a State has traditionally viewed a particular practice as immoral is not

II. The Fourteenth Amendment, 1868

sufficient reason for upholding a law prohibiting the practice; neither history nor tradition could save a law prohibiting miscegenation from constitutional attack. Second, individual decisions by married persons, concerning the intimacies of their physical relationship, even when not intended to produce offspring, are a form of "liberty" protected by the Due Process Clause of the Fourteenth Amendment. Moreover, this protection extends to intimate choices by unmarried as well as married persons." (The Making of a Justice: Reflections on My First 94 Years, Justice Paul Stevens, Little Brown and Company, 2019. Dissenting Opinion of Bowers v. Hardwick, by Associate Justice John Paul Stevens p. 405).

"I of course had dissented in *Bowers*, noting, among other things, that "[a]though the meaning of the principle that 'all men are created equal' is not always clear, it surely must mean that every free citizen has the same interest in 'liberty' that the members of the majority share. From the standpoint of the individual, the homosexual and the heterosexual have the same interest in deciding how he will live his own life, and, more narrowly, how he will conduct himself in his personal and voluntary associations with his companions. State intrusion into the private conduct of either is equally burdensome. "My dissent in *Bowers* was such instance, and though it was unfortunate that *Bowers* remained on the books so long, I took great satisfaction when it was finally overruled." (The Making of a Justice: Reflections on My First 94 Years, Justice Paul Stevens, Little Brown and Company, 2019, p. 403-404).

The wise opinion of Justice Stevens and the members of this court that shared in his dissenting opinion in *Bowers*, and the concurring opinion in *Lawrence* remains to me, an unconstitutional astounding moment.

There is a sense of liberty that pertains to these two cases in 1986 and 2003. It is not founded anywhere in the Fourteenth Amendment. This amendment is an affirmation, not of sex or same sex basis of equality. This sense of liberty is founded in our original bill of rights, where we are all created equal under law and there are certain rights that belong to the people and not in the hands of the government both federal and state.

Yes, it is tragic and unfortunate that a governing majority in a sovereign State has viewed these actions as immoral and unruly. I will shut down the 1986 majority opinion of Justice White and the 2003 majority opinion of Justice Kennedy with two words that truly match this issue...Ninth Amendment. I do not particularly care what the majority or minority of likeminded people think about abortion, same-sex consensual relationships or same-sex marriage. It is not for most of a state or a state assembly to hold an opinion on this manner. The only opinion that matters much is the opinion of the American individual.

The Federal Constitution does not state any statement of homosexuality or sodomy. The Constitution does state the will of the individual to govern for themselves under the protection and safety of their state therein they reside. It is the will of the individual to elect their state representation to represent them within the will of the constitution. With this court ruling of *Bowers*, it is a shame that the defendants pleaded on a violation on their Eighth and Fourteenth Amendments. They did not protest a Ninth Amendment challenge.

"Sodomy was forbidden by laws of the original thirteen states when they ratified the Bill of Rights. In 1868, when the Fourteenth Amendment was ratified, all but five of the 37 states had criminal sodomy laws. Until 1961, all 50 states outlawed sodomy, and today, 24 states and the District of Columbia continue to provide criminal penalties for sodomy

II. The Fourteenth Amendment, 1868

performed in private and between consenting adults." (Opinion of Bowers v. Hardwick, Associate Justice Byron White, 1984).

Criminal sodomy statutes in effect in 1868:

- Alabama: Ala. Rev. Code S 3604 (1867)
- Arkansas: Ark. Stat. ch. 51, Art. IV. S 5 (1868)
- California: 1 Cal. Gen. Laws, para. 1450. S 48 (1865)
- Connecticut: Conn. Gen. Stat., Tit. 122. Ch. 7, S 124 (1866)
- Delaware: Del. Rev. Stat., ch. 131, S 7 (1893)
- Florida: Fla. Rev. Stat., div. 5S 2614 (passed 1868) (1892)
- Georgia: GA. Code SS 4286, 42874290 (1867)
- Illinois: IL. Rev. Stat., div. 5, SS 49, 50 (1845)
- Kansas: (Terr). Kan. Stat., ch. 53, S 7 (1855)
- Kentucky: 1 Ky. Rev. Stat., Crimes and Offences, S 5 (1860)
- Louisiana: La. Rev. Stat., ch. 28, Art IV. S 4 (1856)
- Maine: Me. Rev. Stat., Tit. XII., Ch. 160, S 4 (1840)
- Maryland: 1 Md. Code, Art. 30, S 201 (1860)
- Massachusetts: Mass. Gen. Stat., ch. 165, S 18 (1860)
- Michigan: Mich. Rev. Stat., Tit 30, ch. 158, S 16 (1846)
- Minnesota: Minn. Stat., ch. 96, S 13 (1859)
- Mississippi: Miss. Rev. Code, ch. 64, S LII, Art. 238 (1857)
- Missouri: Mo. Rev. Stat., ch. 50, Art. VIII, S 7 (1856)
- Nebraska: Neb. Rev. Stat., Crim. Code, ch. 4, S 47 (1866)
- Nevada: Nev. Comp. Laws, 1861-1900, Cri. Code, ch. 4, S 47 (1866)
- New Hampshire: N. H. Laws, Act. Of June 19, 1812, S 5, (1815)
- New Jersey: N. J. Rev. Stat., Tit. 8, ch. 1, S 9 (1847)

The Amendments

- New York: N. Y. Rev. Stat., pt. 4, ch. 1, Tit. 5, S. 20 (5th ed. 1859)
- North Carolina: N. C. Rev. Code, ch. 34, S 6 (1855)
- Oregon: Laws of Ore., Crimes – Against Morality, etc., ch. 7, S 655 (1874)
- Pennsylvania: Act of Mar. 31, 1860, S 32, Pub. L. 392, in 1 Digest of Statute Law of Pa. 1700-1903, p. 1011 (Purdon 1905).
- Rhode Island: R. I. Gen. Stat., ch. 232, S 12 (1872)
- South Carolina: Act of 1712, in 2 stat. at Large of S. C. 1682-1716, p. 493 (1837)
- Tennessee: Tenn. Code, ch. 8, Art. 1, S 4843 (1858)
- Texas: Tex. Rev. Stat., Tit. 10, ch 5, Art. 342 (1887) (passed 1860)
- Vermont: Acts and Laws of the State of Vt. (1779)
- Virginia: Va. Code, ch. 149, s 12 (1868)
- West Virginia: W. Va. Code, ch. 149, S 12 (1868)

(Opinion of Bowers v. Hardwick, Associate Justice Byron White, 1984)

The figure that Justice White gave that five states did not criminalize sodomy appears to be incorrect. I count four states: Indiana, Ohio, Iowa, and Wisconsin. It is the right and will of a sovereign state to enact laws in which do not contradict the constitution and to solely protect their citizens of any injustices.

No matter what your religious or private interest convictions are, it must never present itself with racism and prejudice to society. We need to make sure that no public funds are used to discourage one group and give privilege to the other. We must all live in this union of sovereign states and must prevail as one American society.

This matter is an individual and state power, not a centralized power. If by 1868, there were four or five states that did

II. The Fourteenth Amendment, 1868

not criminalize sodomy, then more states should follow suit or not follow suit. In those times, the central power left it up to the states. Did we ever see the federal government criminalize states that did not criminalize acts of sodomy or reward states that did? No, the central power knew its place and knew when not to interfere in matters that belong to the states.

"This is essentially not a question of personal 'preferences' but rather of the legislative authority of the state. I find nothing in the Constitution depriving a state of the power to enact the statute challenged here." (Concurring Opinion of Bowers v. Hardwick, Chief Justice Warren Burger, 1984).

The concurrence opinion of Justice Powell does not raise the issue of state sovereignty. He raises the question to see if the Eighth Amendment was in clear violation. The Eighth Amendment states, "Excessive bail shall not be required, nor excessive fines imposed, nor cruel and unusual punishment inflicted." The Eighth Amendment is a protection that clearly means, "Let the punishment fit the crime." The Founding Fathers wanted justice served, but properly and fairly. They wanted the punishment to fit the crime. The defendants of this case were indeed to include in their case an Eighth Amendment violation. But this case was more than just a violation of punishment of a private act that was violated to an unjust state law.

"This is not to suggest, however, that respondent may not be protected by the Eighth Amendment of the Constitution. The Georgia Statute at issue in this case, Ga. Code Ann. S 16-6-2 (1984), authorizes a court to imprison a person for up to 20 years for a single private, consensual act of sodomy." (Concurrence Opinion of Bowers v. Hardwick, Associate Justice Lewis Powell, 1984).

Of course, the defendants would be protected under the Eighth Amendment. For this type of criminal statute, the punishment seemed a bit severe and unjust.

The Amendments

The only reason Powell brought this issue on his concurrence was due to the dissenting opinion of Associate Justice Harry Blackmun. He brings up three issues that the court should have taken under consideration for this case -- the Eighth Amendment, Ninth Amendment, and the Equal Protection Clause of the Fourteenth Amendment. We know that the court was not going to listen to this case under the Eighth Amendment because the defendants were not even tried, convicted, and sentenced. But still, what the highest court of the land should have done is to send a recommendation to the state of Georgia to review the current statute and to see if it did violate the Eighth Amendment.

Then comes the Equal Protection Clause of the Fourteenth Amendment. The progressive movement loves to twist and turn the verbiage of this amendment's language. I have said it before and continue saying it, the Fourteenth Amendment was written just after the Civil War and to bring equality under law for those newly made persons of black race. This amendment was to interpret a sense of equality under the law across this union. The United States of America did not fight a civil war based on the sexual preference of our persons. Yes, these defendants were indeed violated for a denial of their due process under the Sixth Amendment. But also, for an invasion of their right to privacy under the following a Ninth amendment violation.

Now consider the Ninth Amendment that states, "The enumeration in the Constitution, of certain rights, shall not be construed to deny or disparage others retained by the people." Does the Ninth include sexual orientation and sexual preference? Yes, and it is up to the individual or individuals residing in their state herein to define their laws with accordance to the constitution. Would the high court find enough precedent to assist these two individuals sought fair and free

II. The Fourteenth Amendment, 1868

justice in a ninth amendment violation? The equal protection clause of Amendment Fourteen did not fit their narrative as we all know that the Fourteenth does not constitute sexual orientation violation.

I feel for the defendants that had to endure the cruelty and harassment of the law enforcement of Georgia and similar law enforcement statutes of sodomy. But if they wanted to have the law changed, reformed, or repealed. The correct way in going about it, is to petition their state legislature to consider it, not the courts. But fortunately, the citizenship of Michael Hardwick has the same rights and liberties as any heterosexual person. His rights have been violated not by the Fourteenth Amendment based on his white race, but by his stance on his ninth amendment based on his private sexual preference and orientation in his right to privacy.

* * *

The case that overturned *Bowers* was the 2003 *Lawrence v. Texas* ruling. The Texas state legislature passed an anti-sodomy law. This court case was filed by an adult homosexual white male with a young adult black male who were arrested and convicted for having sexual intercourse in the privacy of the place of residence. The Supreme Court did not declare "homosexuality a fundamental right" but instead declared that the legislation was a violation of the right to privacy as stated in the 1965 court ruling of *Griswold v. Connecticut*.

If the 1965 opinion of *Griswold v. Connecticut* stated that a judgment against an act in the bedroom was a violation of the "right to privacy," then how come it was never applied in the 1984 case.

"John Lawrence was convicted of violating a Texas statute making it a crime for two persons of the same sex to engage in certain intimate sexual conduct and fined $200

The Amendments

plus court costs. After the Texas Court of Appeals upheld the conviction, we granted Lawrence's petition for certiorari to address three question: (1) whether the conviction violated the Equal Protection Clause; (2) whether it deprived him of "liberty" protected by the Due Process Clause; (3) whether the Court's 1986 decision in Bowers v. Hardwick should be overruled." (The Making of a Justice: Reflections on My First 94 Years, Justice Paul Stevens, Little Brown and Company, 2019, p. 403).

Please see page 143 in my explanation in how wrong the most senior member of our American Supreme Court was in his 1986 *Bowers* dissent as much as his concurring opinion on 2003 *Lawrence*.

The state law in Texas as the state law in Georgia is not a violation on a Fourteenth Amendment challenge. These laws and like other states are a clear violation of a Ninth Amendment challenge. The individuals charged in these cases are being deprived of "liberty", not from the affirmed Fourteenth, but on the liberty deprival of the Fourth, Fifth, Sixth Amendments, and most importantly Ninth Amendment.

"My dissent in *Bowers* was such instance, and though it was unfortunate that *Bowers* remained on the books so long, I took great satisfaction when it was finally overruled." (The Making of a Justice: Reflections on My First 94 Years, Justice Paul Stevens, Little Brown and Company, 2019, p. 403-404).

My opinion of *Bowers* was such instance, and though it was unfortunate that *Bowers* remained on the books for so long on the wrong amendment challenge. I took great disappointment when it was finally overruled on the wrong constitutional precedent.

Justice Sandra Day O'Connor's concurrence opinion claim that this law was a violation of the equal protection clause to the Fourteenth Amendment. You do not need a reassurance of the Fourteenth Amendment, if we are all covered in

II. The Fourteenth Amendment, 1868

our bill of rights protections. The Fourteenth Amendment applies to the race of an American person. It is written in the language and in its American history.

The opinion of the court by Kennedy, Stevens, Souter, Ginsburg, Breyer, and O'Connor overturned *Bowers v. Hardwick*, stated:

"In our tradition the State is not omnipresent in the home. And there are other spheres of our lives and existence, outside the home, where the State should not be a dominant presence." (Opinion of Lawrence v. Texas, 2003 by Associate Justice Anthony Kennedy).

There should never be an omnipresent of any type of government, both federal and state in the American household. Kennedy begins his opinion as a dreamer rather than a constitutionalist. The states, or respectively the people, have the right to enact such laws to protect, not disparaged each person of the state they reside.

Kennedy continued the opinion by saying:

"Freedom extends beyond spatial bounds. Liberty presumes an autonomy of self that includes freedom of thought, belief, expression, and certain intimate conduct. The instant case involves liberty of the person both in its spatial and more transcendent dimensions." (Opinion of Lawrence v. Texas, 2003 by Associate Justice Anthony Kennedy).

Parts of this opinion sound like a political poem rather than a legal precedent or true opinion brief. Kennedy stated that yes, this country has freedom and liberty based on the Bill of Rights in the Constitution, the Ninth Amendment comes to mind.

Since the inception of the Ninth and Tenth Amendments, American persons on all sides of the question of same-sex and sodomy have seen victories and they have seen defeats. There have been plebiscites, legislation, persuasion, and loud voices — in other words, a representative republic.

The Amendments

"Victories in one place for some, see North Carolina Const., Amdt. 1 (providing that "[m]arriage between one man and one woman is the only domestic legal union that shall be valid or recognized in this state") (approved by a popular vote, 61% to 39% on May 8, 2012), are offset victories in other places for others, see Maryland Question 6 (establishing "that Maryland's civil marriage laws allow gay and lesbian couples to obtain a civil marriage license") (approved by a popular vote, 52% to 48%, om November 6, 2012.). Compare Maine Question 1 (permitting "the state of Maine to issue marriage licenses to same-sex couples") (approved by a popular vote of 53% to 47%, on November 6, 2012) with Maine Question 1 (rejecting "the new law that lets same-sex couples marry"), (Scalia's Court, Kevin A. Ring, 2004, 2016, Justice Scalia dissent on Windsor v. US, p. 392).

"We might have let the people decide," (Scalia's Court, Kevin A. Ring, 2004, 2016, Justice Scalia dissent on Windsor v. US, p. 293).

In Maryland, they had a plebiscite to allow homosexual couples to obtain a marriage license. Did anybody challenge that? No. Because the state, or respectively the people, were the ones in charge of passing their own legislation. In a way, this nation has become tolerant on the issue on same-sex marriage but not tolerant to other forms of marriages or consensual relationships.

We want the individual within their own state to respect the laws/rules of federalism and let the people pass any legislative measure they see fit if it does not contradict with the federal constitution.

"Most of today's opinion has no relevance to its actual holding — that the Texas statute "furthers no legitimate state interest which can justify its application to petitioners under rational-basis review." (Scalia's Court, Kevin A. Ring, 2004, 2016, page 358, Scalia's dissent on Lawrence v. TX).

II. The Fourteenth Amendment, 1868

It is whatever most of these states' constituents elect -- a majority legislative body to have their views represented by the distinguished legislative members. But sometimes there is a small minority group of American persons' rights and protections might be denied. We shall never forget the minority of voters as we support the majority of voters.

"... nowhere does the Court's opinion declare that homosexual sodomy is a "fundamental right" under the Due Process Clause; nor does it subject the Texas law to the standard review that would be appropriate (strict scrutiny) if homosexual sodomy were a "fundamental right." (Scalia's Court, Kevin A. Ring, 2004, 2016, page 358, Scalia's dissent on Lawrence v. TX).

The majority opinion as well as the dissenting opinions of this case fails to understand all the bill of rights. Homosexuality and sodomy and even heterosexuality is a fundamental right embedded in our Ninth Amendment explaining the sense of the individual right.

Justice Thomas made a short but to the point dissenting opinion.

"If I were a member of the Texas Legislature, I would vote to repeal it." (Dissenting Opinion of Lawrence v. Texas, 2003 by Associate Justice Clarence Thomas).

What does Justice Clarence Thomas mean by this statement? It clearly means that he wanted to give this legislation back to Texas for review, reform, or repeal. He and the other members of the Supreme Court are not legislators, they are jurists. But when there is an unjust and unconstitutional state directive or federal directive...it is the job of the high court to root it out to set a rightful and correct interpretation into a constitutional precedence. This Texas law if applied incorrectly, can have a negative impact upon the other sovereign states. All persons based on sex, sexual identity, sexual orientation, and marital or consensual relationships are applied by the Ninth Amendment to our federal constitution. That all fifty sovereign states of this American union have entered a constitutional compact to enjoy these rights for persons as well as states. These rights are not based on a Fourteenth Amendment precedence... in that the high court has interpreted incorrectly. And I hope that one day they will rule it correctly on its original and finest precedence...the Ninth Amendment.

The three branches of the federal government have truly reshaped our republic into a quite a mess of unorthodox interpretations. Some We the People, in other words, We the Individual understand the language of the Fourteenth Amendment and how it was meant to be interpreted. After the civil war, our republic began to reshape to a rightful place in the world to disassociate ourselves from the wrath of slavery. While maintaining our other liberties and rights for our other American persons.

Somehow, the general government started to make a mockery of our newly added Fourteenth Amendment and created new outlandish interpretations that were not consistent with the authors of this article.

The Fourteenth Amendment means what it says and says what it means, while the other amendments mean what they say. We must look correctly to each amendment to define equally the individuality of the American person.

E. Life Relations

The matter of life of an American person has been the sense of life, liberty, and the pursuit of happiness. As promised in the Declaration of Independence and within the 1787 Constitution. The purpose of respecting the life of the American person is that liberty is a precious thing for the individual. The bill of rights is the guaranteed protections for the individual American. The Fourteenth Amendment is the affirmation to those protections for the American person.

There have been violations to the human lifestyle of the American individual from of course the slavery days to the unfortunate following of the eugenics movement.

One example of a state law and unfortunately affirmed by the union's high court that is a serious violation of our persons' rights happened in the Commonwealth of Virginia.

The Virginia Sterilization Act of 1924 and the Virginia Racial Integrity Act of 1924, both pieces of legislation to be supported by a degenerate organization of eugenics. In order to place white supremacist policies upon this union from these degenerate individuals were encroaching on other persons' bill of rights.

What is even more outrageous is that this case went all the way up to the Supreme Court of the United States and a majority of eight justices voted to uphold this Virginia

The Amendments

legislative statute and crush down the entire system of bill of rights protections.

Carrie Buck, a young, white lady sued the State Colony for Epileptics and Feebleminded for violating her equal justice under the law rights as an American individual.

"Carrie Buck is a feeble-minded white woman who was committed to the State Colony above mentioned in due form. She is the daughter of a feeble-minded mother in the same institution, and the mother of an illegitimate feeble-minded child." (Opinion Brief of Buck v. Bell, 1927 by Associate Justice Oliver Wendell Holmes).

I would say Justice Oliver Wendell Holmes, appointed by Theodore Roosevelt, would have to be the second despised associate justice to the high court, right after Chief Justice Roger Taney.

"An Act of Virginia approved March 20, 1924 (Laws 1924, c. 394) recites that the health of the patient and the welfare of society may be promoted in certain cases by the sterilization of mental defectives, under careful safeguard, etc.; that the sterilization may be effected in males by vasectomy and in females by salpingectomy, without serious pain or substantial danger to life; that the Commonwealth is supporting in various institutions many defective persons who if now discharged would become *206 a menace but if incapable of procreating might be discharged with safety and become self-supporting with benefit to themselves and to society; and that experience has shown heredity plays an important part in the transmission of insanity, imbecility, etc. The statute then enacts that whenever the superintendent of certain institutions including the abovenamed State Colony shall be of opinion that it is for the best interest of the patients and of society that an inmate under his care should be sexually sterilized, he may have the operation performed upon any patient afflicted with hereditary forms insanity, imbecility,

II. The Fourteenth Amendment, 1868

etc., on complying with the very careful provisions by which the act protects the patients from possible abuse." (Opinion Brief of Buck v. Bell, 1927 by Associate Justice Oliver Wendell Holmes).

It is not the right or power of a government, federal and state to offer any type of protective custody to an American person without the sense of due process. As it is stated in the Sixth Amendment and affirmed in Amendment Fourteen.

In reading what this Virginia legislative act has been brought against Virginia persons, and individuals of other states that have passed similar legislation, is shameful and contradictory to the federal constitution. Eight shameful jurists have given authority to a sole bureaucrat to order the sexual sterilization of an American person just because of a mental disability. It is a similar ruling to when eight jurists gave permission to a Pennsylvania bureaucrat the right to decide a woman's "right" to terminate a pregnancy, *Planned Parenthood of SE PA v. Casey,* 1992.

"It is better for all the world, if instead of waiting to execute degenerate offspring for crime, or to let them starve for their imbecility, society can prevent those who are manifestly unfit from continuing their kind. The principle that sustains compulsory vaccination is broad enough to cover cutting the Fallopian tubes. Jacobson v. Massachusetts, 197 U.S. 11, 25 S. Ct. 358, 49 L. Ed. 643, 3 Ann. Cas. 765. Three generations of imbeciles are enough." (Opinion Brief of Buck v. Bell, 1927 by Associate Justice Oliver Wendell Holmes).

"Three generations of imbeciles are enough." – Justice Oliver Wendell Holmes. A very despicable, and surreal statement towards our American liberties and rights.

This is just one violation of a government entity that has presented to deny the persons' equal rights under the law and protections of their bill of rights and affirmed by the Fourteenth Amendment. The Fourteenth Amendment is a legislative and executive tool of enforcement towards an abusive federal and/or state governments. But what people are trying to portray the Fourteenth as a savior article is far from the truth. Citizens, politicians, and individuals are focusing their might on a Fourteenth Amendment challenge where they should focus on a bill of rights challenge.

* * *

We saw the governments within state governments and the federal high court deny due process and a life of liberty and happiness to many persons across this union of sovereign states. This act on the human dignity of life was an attack on our constitutional principles.

Then came the 1965 ruling of *Griswold v. Connecticut*, in where unfortunately the rule of privacy and the Ninth Amendment first aired its senses to the union. It is a shame people and politicians have not fully read the ENTIRE constitution prior to 1965. Even today's culture, we could have had just, and correct rulings based on each constitutional guaranteed rights and protections.

Then came in 1973 and later in 1992 a federal high court ruling that not only attacked the sense of the right of the individual. But an attack on the rules of federalism that governs this republic. The Fourteenth Amendment reshaped America for the better good of our republic, but somehow these rulings' interpretation of the Fourteenth reshaped oddly our American union of sovereign states' republic.

* * *

"The States may, if they wish, permit abortion on demand, but the Constitution does not require them to do so. The permissibility of abortion, and the limitations upon it, are to be resolved like most

II. The Fourteenth Amendment, 1868

important questions in our democracy: by persons trying to persuade one another and then voting."

– Associate Justice Antonin Scalia

"My view is, regardless, of whether if you think prohibiting abortion is good or if you think prohibiting is bad...regardless of what you come out on that. My only point is the constitution does not say anything about it. It leaves it up to democratic choice, some states have prohibited it, some states didn't, what *Roe v. Wade* said that no state can prohibit it...that is simply not in the constitution, it was one of those many things, most things in the world, left to democratic choice."

– Associate Justice Antonin Scalia on Piers Morgan, 2012

"Democratic choice," in other words, I rather would have put them differently and federalism succinctly. Individuals seeking liberty choices against an oppressive federal government and/or state governments. It is stated in our Ninth Amendment, and before the Tenth Amendment.

The late Associate Justice Antonin Scalia were one of the few, and always was too quick to pull out the Ninth and Tenth Amendment protections towards the American individual. Very few jurists today on the high court vaguely even mentioned our individual rights, let alone only cite the Tenth Amendment.

Although, Justice Scalia did not take part in discussing and debating the decision that would lead to a new sense of rights and liberties, not prescribed in our constitution. As we all care about the life situation of the unborn, we must not forget and care in respecting the present life of the person in fighting to preserve their rights and liberties.

The Amendments

If one person's rights are being denied, then all rights will be denied.

"The right to privacy, whether it be founded in the Fourteenth Amendment's concept of personal liberty and restrictions upon state action, as we feel it is, or, as the District Court determined, in the Ninth Amendment's reservation of the rights of the people, is broad enough to encompass a woman's decision whether to terminate her pregnancy." (Opinion Brief of *Roe v. Wade* by Associate Justice Harry Blackmun, 1973).

The high court did find a Ninth Amendment precedence in the discussion of life and abortion within our union of sovereign states. But quite frankly they based it more in the "substantive" due process clause within the Fourteenth, than in the Ninth.

"A state criminal abortion statute of the current Texas type, that excepts from criminality onto a life-saving procedure on behalf of the mother, without regard to pregnancy stage and without recognition of the other interests involved, is violative of the Due Process Clause of the Fourteenth Amendment." (Opinion Brief of *Roe v. Wade* by Associate Justice Harry Blackmun, 1973).

"To reach its result, the Court necessarily has had to find within the scope of the Fourteenth Amendment a right that was apparently completely unknown to the drafters of the Amendment. As early as 1821, the first state law dealing directly with abortion was enacted by the Connecticut Legislature. By the time of the adoption of the Fourteenth Amendment in 1868, there were at least 36 laws enacted by state or territorial legislatures limiting abortion. While many States have amended or updated their laws on the books in 1868 remain in effect today." (Dissenting Brief of *Roe v. Wade* by Associate Justice Richard Rehnquist, 1973).

II. The Fourteenth Amendment, 1868

Both the majority opinion and dissenting opinions of the high court regarding the case of *Roe v. Wade* are constitutionally wrong. There is already a due process clause in the constitution. It is embedded in the Sixth Amendment. The due process clause of the Fourteenth Amendment is clearly meant for violations involving persons of race or color, not of life or sex. Ms. Norma McCorvey, a.k.a as Jane Roe, already has established rights under her bill of rights, more on the Ninth than on the Fourteenth. This ruling and further state legislature statutes further reshaped the republic to an unprecedented unconstitutional mess. We should all respect the views and opinions and livelihood of Americans… and it should be done via-constitutionally appropriated.

The *Roe* decision, later the *Dobbs* decision should not have been focused in being about a life issue, or a pro-choice issue. All common sense constitutional minded Americans know it is regarding a liberty issue that affects all Americans. A liberty issue embedded in our bill of rights.

* * *

Another ruling over the abortion issue in which the high court sided a partial overturned precedent of *Roe* and against the sense of liberty was the infamous abortion case *Planned Parenthood of South Eastern Pennsylvania v. Casey 1992.*

"My views on this matter are unchanged from those I set forth in my separate opinions in *Webster v. Reproductive Health Services* and *Ohio v. Akron Center for Reproductive Health.* The states may, if they wish, permit abortion on demand, but the Constitution does not *require* them to do so. The permissibility of abortion, and the limitations upon it, are to be resolved like most important questions in our democracy: by persons trying to persuade on another and

The Amendments

then voting." (Scalia's Court, Kevin A. Ring, 2004, 2016, Scalia's dissent on Planned Parenthood SE PA v. Casey, p. 193).

I would like to point out to my readers, where in the Constitution states that, "Abortion is allowed and that no state should be allowed to prohibit it."

The answer is that no such statement exists in this document that still governs our country. Whom would you rather rule this great land of ours, your voice in the state legislature, nine unelected lawyers, or the individual-minded person? I will take the voice of the individual first over a quorum of state legislators, or over these nine unelected jurists. It is the voice of the individual, respectively the people that get to decide for these decisions. The state legislature will give their input but only under the guidance of the individual person, as placed on its Ninth Amendment doctrine. Neither on *Roe* nor on *Casey* does the court grant this abortion right truly on the ninth amendment.

"... the best the Court can do to explain how it is that the word "liberty" must be thought to include the right to destroy human fetuses is to rattle off a collection of adjectives that simply decorate a value judgment and conceal a political choice.", (Scalia's Court, Kevin A. Ring, 2004, 2016, Scalia's dissent on Planned Parenthood SE PA v. Casey, p. 107).

The high court, in this case and other cases, sometimes loves to reinvent words and extend their vocabulary to fulfill their own personal agenda and to inflict it upon the rest of us by force and against the will of the individual.

"In this court's opinion, the majority used the term *stare decisis* to achieve their objective. This term — which means the practice of adhering to precedent — was especially important in this case because the issue was divisive and because so many people had come to rely on the legality of abortion," (Scalia's Court, Kevin A. Ring, 2004, 2016, pp. 101-102).

II. The Fourteenth Amendment, 1868

The majority were so scared that this case would overrule a long-standing ruling known as *Roe v. Wade* that they decided to ignore states' and individual autonomous rights to still maintain that 1973 ruling on the books and declare this one out into the garbage. Scalia gave a convincing dissent upon the court's view on *stare decisis*, also known as "central holding."

Central holding of a lawful case by a central government branch is not the vision the framers had when creating the rules and judicial procedures for the court system. There are certain cases need to be federally managed, life issues pertaining to the medical procedure of abortion resides with the individual and the state that individual herein resides.

"The Court's reliance upon *stare decisis* can best be described as contrived. It insists upon the necessity of adhering not to all of *Roe*, but only to what it calls "central holding." It seems to me that *stare decisis* ought to be applied even to the doctrine of stare decisis, and I confess never to have heard of this new, keep-what-you-want-and-throw-the-rest-version. I wonder whether, as applied of *Marbury v. Madison*, for example, the new version of *stare decisis* would be satisfied if we allowed courts to review the constitutionality of only those statutes that (like the one in *Marbury*) pertain to the jurisdiction of the courts." (Scalia's Court, Kevin A. Ring, 2004, 2016, Scalia's dissent on Planned Parenthood SE PA v. Casey, pp. 114-115).

This is the perfect example of how progressive jurists have applied, or in this case not applied, constitutional basis on the law being examined by the court. Most of the court's ruling was like cutting up a barbecued steak and saying, "This part is good, this part is bad." I am sorry to say but that is never how a jurist, a person of the law, is supposed to interpret the law. Either interpret as is or recuse yourself. I am going to show you a few excerpts and my opinions on

The Amendments

the Opinion and Dissenting brief on *Planned Parenthood SE PA v. Casey.*
"The majority opinion of the high court concluded that in "Part V-E that all of the statute's recordkeeping and reporting requirements, except that relating to spousal notice, are constitutional. The reporting provision relating to the reasons a married woman has not notified her husband that she intends to have an abortion must be invalidated because it places an undue burden on a woman's choice." (Opinion Brief on Planned Parenthood SE PA v. Casey, Associate Justice Sandra Day O'Connor 1992).
It is a sad day for America that we take in the word of a bureaucrat over the right of the individual and families. I am not surprised since the court ruling of *Wickard v. Filburn.* The court sought to give more power to the central government over the states and respectively to the people. The progressive movement has made their quest to destroy the American nuclear family and bring distortion and disharmony to the family circle. What kind of a nation have we become that a married woman cannot have a family discussion with her husband in a matter of her pregnancy because it is now invalidated and forbidden by a decree of the central power. How dare they, I ask! Why are these jurists interfering in the private lives of American families? Why are even politicians interfering in the lives of the American individual?

"The Roe Court reached too far when it analogized the right to abort a fetus to the rights involved in *Pierce v. Society of Sisters, 268 U.S. 510, 69 L. Ed. 1070 , 45 S. Ct. 571; Meyer v. Nebraska, 262 U.S. 390, 67 L. Ed. 1042, 43 S. Ct. 625; Loving v. Virginia, 388 U.S. 1, 18 L. Ed. 2d 1010, 87 S. Ct. 1817;* and *Griswold v. Connecticut, 381 U.S. 479, 14 L. Ed. 2d 510, 85 S. Ct. 1678,* and thereby deemed the right to abortion to be "fundamental." None of these decisions endorsed an all-encompassing "right to privacy" as *Roe,*

II. The Fourteenth Amendment, 1868

supra at 152-153, claimed. Because abortion involves the purposeful termination of potential life, the abortion decision must be recognized as *sui generis*, different kind from the rights protected in the earlier cases under the rubric of personal or family privacy and autonomy." (Dissenting Brief on Planned Parenthood SE PA v. Casey, Chief Justice William Rehnquist, 1992).

I am not familiar with the *Pierce v. Society of Sisters; Meyer v. Nebraska* rulings but the ones that I am familiar with are *Loving v. Virginia and Griswold v. Connecticut.* With the ruling of *Loving*, it can be most definitely be a violation of the due process clause of the Fourteenth Amendment as well as the Sixth Amendment. For Griswold, it was stated as a right to privacy under the Ninth Amendment, a guaranteed right protection for the individual.

Neither *Roe*, nor *Casey* rulings were ruled on the true precedent violation of the Ninth Amendment.

"And the historical traditions of the American - - as evidenced by the English common law and by the American abortion statutes in existence both at the time of the Fourteenth Amendment's adoption and *Roe's* issuance - - do not support the view that the right to terminate one's pregnancy is "fundamental." (Dissenting Brief on Planned Parenthood SE PA v. Casey, Chief Justice William Rehnquist, 1992).

The dissenters of this brief are quite accurate. The Fourteenth Amendment was presented to Congress right after the Civil War. A war that was fought to bring clarity on the race relations of this union. The proponents of the legislation were looking to pass a law to protect the rights of all Americans based on race and color. They were not looking to protect the rights of a female individual trying to end her pregnancy. So, let us put this debate to an end. There is nothing in the Constitution, in THE AMENDMENTS, the declaration of "the right of a fetus." There is the right of

The Amendments

the individual and the right of a sovereign state, but never a right to a fetus.

"The correct analysis is that which is set forth by the plurality opinion in Webster, supra: A woman's interest in having an abortion is a form of liberty protected by the Due Process Clause, but states may regulate abortion procedures in ways rationally related to a legitimate state interest. P. 966." (Dissenting Brief on Planned Parenthood SE PA v. Casey, Chief Justice William Rehnquist, 1992).

In paraphrasing Scalia's words during an interview with TV commentator Piers Morgan, "Regardless if you think prohibiting abortion is good or bad, the Constitution does not say anything about it. It leaves it up to democratic choice, some states have prohibited, others have not, what *Roe v. Wade* stated is that no state can prohibit, and that simply is not in the Constitution." If the court ruling of 1973 made it clear that no state can prohibit it, fine, but it did not state that no state can regulate an abortion procedure. It is not in the best lawful and constitutional interest for the federal government or state governments to regulate this issue. It is there to be regulated by the self-reliant individual person to determine if they want to proceed with the pregnancy or terminate the pregnancy.

"The dissenting opinion of the court concluded "that a woman's decision to abort her unborn child is not a constitutionally protected "liberty" because (1) the Constitution says absolutely nothing about it, and (2) the longstanding traditions of American society have permitted it to be legally proscribed. See e. g., *Ohio v. Akron Center for Reproductive Health, 497 U.S. 502, 520, 111 L. Ed. 2d 405, 110 S. Ct. 2972*. The Pennsylvania statute should be upheld in its entirety under rational basis test. Pp. 979-981." (Dissenting Brief on Planned Parenthood SE PA v. Casey, Chief Justice William Rehnquist, 1992).

II. The Fourteenth Amendment, 1868

The state law of Pennsylvania is quite clear. The state is not banning or prohibiting an abortion procedure. It is simply just regulating the abortion medical procedure. But again, the federal government and several state governments are ignoring the will of the Ninth Amendment. The Fourteenth Amendment's due process clause does not enter this discussion. To make it blatantly and constitutionally clear. If the medical procedure went wrong, and the individual's rights have been violated. Then a challenge on the bill of rights is best suited than a Fourteenth challenge.

And now comes an end of an era in where the issue of abortion was tested again in the courts. And once again, the topic was focused on being a life or pro-choice decision issue. Nothing could be further from the truth and once again, politicians; jurists; media pundits; and several individual persons were bamboozled in believing s false right or negated right, not mentioned in the constitution.

On December 1, 2021, the case of *Dobbs v. Jackson Women's Health Organization* was heard to determine this life, pro-choice issue once again in open court and in the open court of unruly public opinion. And once yet again, the high court and the court of popular opinion came together in disagreement against the Constitution in its official question on individual rights.

* * *

Dobbs v. Jackson Women's Health Organization, 2022 silenced the constitutional common sense for the many and praised the ignorance for the few.

"Mississippi's Gestational Age Act provides that "[e]xcept in a medical emergency or in the case of a severe fetal abnormality, a person shall not intentionally or knowingly perform…or induce an abortion of an unborn human being

The Amendments

if the probable gestational age of the unborn human being has been determined to be greater than fifteen (15) weeks." Miss. Code Ann. Section 41-41-191." (Syllabus of Dobbs v. Jackson Women's Health Organization, 2022).

> The high court held: "The Constitution does not confer a right to abortion; *Roe* and *Casey* are overruled; and the authority to regulate abortion is returned to the people and their elected representatives."
> (Syllabus of Dobbs v. Jackson Women's Health Organization, 2022).

Take it for the Magnolia state to deny a person's rights under the Constitution's bill of rights. I am not surprised one bit that this time it was the great state of Mississippi and not the Lone Star state...Texas. This is not a question if the unborn from date of conception to the 9-month birth stage is a human being or not. The federal government or state governments are not here to make this assumption or decision. Yes, this case was applied judicial review, but it was reviewed erroneously.

The high court of the land held regarding this case that the Constitution does not specifically confer a right to abortion. They are right and they are wrong. The high court also held that the authority to regulate abortion is returned to the people and their elected representatives. They are half-right and half-wrong.

> "The enumeration in the Constitution, of certain rights, shall not be construed to deny or disparage others retained by the people."
> The Ninth Amendment, Bill of Rights of our Constitution

II. The Fourteenth Amendment, 1868

It is up to the individual in which they reside in their state of residency to define and decree their rights. If it is not listed in the Constitution as a right, which is not as we all clearly know. Then all constitutional common-sense Americans know that it is listed to be defined in our Ninth Amendment.

I have no patience for members of our judiciary branch from state and federal lower courts to upper courts to be emotional rather than constitutional. Associate Justice Samuel Alito is no exception to this rule. He writes with emotions to the law rather with the constitution to the law.

"Abortion presents a profound moral issue on which Americans hold sharply conflicting views." (Opinion Brief of Dobbs v. Jackson Women's Health Organization, Associate Justice Samuel Alito, 2022).

Abortion *DOES NOT* present a moral issue. It presents a constitutional issue. It is not the duty of a government, both federal or state to decree what is moral and not moral to its persons. That is *NOT* written in the Constitution.

"Some believe fervently that a human person comes into being at conception and that abortion ends an innocent life. Others feel just as strongly that any regulation of abortion invades a woman's right to control her own body and prevents women from achieving full equality. Still others in a third group think that abortion should be allowed under some but not all circumstances, and those within this group hold a variety of views about particular restrictions that should be imposed." (Opinion Brief of Dobbs v. Jackson Women's Health Organization, Associate Justice Samuel Alito, 2022).

Where am I in this census given by the high court? I am not the one who believes that life begins at conception. As I am in favor of an individual American (female) individual to have control of their body. But I do not believe that a (female) individual needs the need to achieve full equality on the issue of abortion. The persons of this nation regarding of the sex or gender, (or gender-change) have obtained full equality of the law. Since they are natural-born, or naturalized, or a person within this union as persons and their rights are founded within our bill of rights. We do not need a substantive Fourteenth affirmation. The Court and the states know this fact but choose to ignore. The Court chose to reshape this marvelous republic to appease to their own special interest minds, just like the decisions of *Dred Scott*, *Plessy*, and *Korematsu*.

I am not in this so-called third group of allowing or not allowing certain circumstances for abortion. Certain people and government cannot impose their way of personal thinking on to another person. This is not how this American republic was founded on. And still to this day, we must respect our individual rights for all.

"For the first 185 years after the adoption of the Constitution, each State was permitted to address this issue in accordance with the views of its persons. Then, in 1973, this Court decided Roe v. Wade, 410 U.S. 113. Even though the Constitution makes no mention of abortion, the Court held that it confers a broad right to obtain one. It did not claim that American law or the common law had ever recognized such a right, and its survey of history ranged from the constitutionality irrelevant (e.g., its discussion of abortion in antiquity) to the plainly incorrect (e.g., its assertion that abortion was probably never a crime under common law). After cataloguing a wealth of information having no bearing in the meaning of the Constitution, the opinion might be found in a statute enacted by a legislature." (Opinion Brief of Dobbs v. Jackson Women's Health Organization, Associate Justice Samuel Alito, 2022).

Since the constitutional's adoption in 1787 and all sovereign states abiding to its will, each Individual and each State has been permitted to address this issue and other

II. The Fourteenth Amendment, 1868

related issues pertaining to the individual's rights under the Ninth Amendment. Justice Alito is only addressing what the majority of persons' voice in their state legislature, but he is choosing to ignore the minority voice of persons. This is where the discussion is brought upon a Ninth Amendment discussion for the better of all persons, not to be decided by the state legislature.

"At the time of Roe, 30 States still prohibited abortion at all stages. In the years prior to that decision, about a third of the States had liberalized their laws, but Roe abruptly ended that political process. It imposed the same highly restrictive regime on the entire Nation, and it effectively struck down the abortion laws of every single State." (Opinion Brief of Dobbs v. Jackson Women's Health Organization, Associate Justice Samuel Alito, 2022).

"It imposed the same highly restrictive regime on the entire Nation."

If the States prior to Roe imposed "the *SAME* highly restrictive regime," then there is a reason that this issue is left up to the individual and not up to the state governments or the federal government. In this American republic of sovereign states, there are no need for imposing highly restrictive regimes on its states or persons. Now that is strictly forbidden in the Constitution.

"As Justice Byron White aptly put it in his dissent, the decision represented the "exercise of raw judicial power," 410 U.S., at 222, and it sparked a national controversy that has embittered our political culture for a half century." (Opinion Brief of Dobbs v. Jackson Women's Health Organization, Associate Justice Samuel Alito, 2022).

Justice Alito quotes from a justice that blatantly has no regard for the right of the individual on their Fourth Amendment right, let along their Ninth Amendment right. Associate Justice Byron White gave a very chilling, unprincipled, and quite unconstitutional opinion in 1968 in favor

The Amendments

of law enforcement and against our bill of rights protections involving due process.

It is only an "exercise of raw judicial power," if we allow jurists of any court to dictate their constitutional opinion upon their own special interest beliefs. Was it "raw judicial power," when the high court stated that a black civilian was unable to become a person and considered a human being? Was it "raw judicial power," when the high court stated that we had to have separate private and public facilities among the races of this country? Was it "raw judicial power," to deny individuals of mentally challenged syndromes of their due process? Was it "raw judicial power," to deny due process of the law and incarcerate Japanese Americans in internment camps? All these high court opinions are in my constitutional opinion raw judicial power and should have never been a constitutional precedent that haunts our republic to this day.

Whether the *Roe* decision was considered a "raw judicial power," it was a decision that was badly interpreted regardless if you believe prohibiting abortion is good, or prohibiting abortion is bad. This decision indeed has reshaped our republic with an unprecedented Fourteenth Amendment interpretation that was never supposed to have this type of interpretation in the history of our republic.

Then came 1992 with another court's oddly reshaping our republic with the matter of abortion.

"Eventually, in *Planned Parenthood of Southeastern Pennsylvania v. Casey*, 505 U.S. 833 (1992), the Court revisited *Roe*, but the Members of the Court split three ways. Two Justices expressed no desire to change *Roe* in any way. Four others wanted to overrule the decision in its entirety. And the three remaining Justices, who jointly signed the following opinion, took a third position. Their opinion did not endorse *Roe's* reasoning, and it even hinted that one or

II. The Fourteenth Amendment, 1868

more of its authors might have "reservations" about whether the Constitution protects a right to abortion. But the opinion concluded that stare decisis, which calls for prior decisions to be followed in most instances, required adherence to what it called *Roe's* "central holding"—that a State may not constitutionally protect fetal life before "visibility"—even if claimed, would undermine respect for this Court and the rule of law." (Opinion Brief of Dobbs v. Jackson Women's Health Organization, Associate Justice Samuel Alito, 2022).

Casey decision was a constitutional sham that brought nothing but reshaped unevenly this republic. If I were a justice during the *Roe* and *Casey* argument and decision, I would be the lone high court jurist applying its true interpretation to these cases. I would express desire to change *Roe* in bringing the appropriate bill of rights challenge, and not the Fourteenth Amendment challenge it sunk into existence. I would not overrule but interpret it clearly so that the federal government and its state governments protect their laws appropriately without damaging our Ninth Amendment right.

Stare Decisis is an evil tool to bring forth an excuse to expand the role of a central (federal) government excess control and funding. To maintain an unconstitutional ruling, they will find ways to compromise it to cover their own special interest abilities. It is quite dangerous to have a jurist with nationalistic or progressive ideals cloud their judgment to interpret our constitution. The Constitution says what it says and means what it says. It is a principled document that dictates what the law should be as written. Many people have different views on it, and it is quite understanding. But in the end, you cannot change the words of the original framers or of the amendment framers.

The Amendments

"The Court's discussion left open at least three ways in which some combination of these provisions could protect the abortion right. One possibility was that the right was "founded... in the Ninth Amendment's reservation of the rights of the people." *Id.*, at 153. Another was that the right was rooted in the First, Fourth, or Fifth Amendment, or in some combination of those provisions, and that this right had been "incorporated" into the Due Process Clause of the Fourteenth Amendment just as many other Bill of Rights provisions had by been incorporated. *Ibid*; see also McDonald v. Chicago, 561 U.S. 742, 763-766 (2010) (majority opinion) (discussing incorporation). And a third path was that the First, Fourth, and Fifth Amendments played no role and that the right was simply a component of the "liberty" protected by the Fourteenth Amendment's Due Process Clause. *Roe* expressed the "fee[ling]" that the Fourteenth Amendment was the provision that did work, but its message seemed to be that the abortion right could be found somewhere in the Constitution and that specifying its exact location was not of paramount importance. The *Casey* Court did not defend this unfocused analysis and instead grounded its decision solely on the "liberty" protected by the Fourteenth Amendment's Due Process Clause." (Opinion Brief of Dobbs v. Jackson Women's Health Organization, Associate Justice Samuel Alito, 2022).

There is no three ways in describing the liberty bill of rights in foretelling the right of an abortion. There is only one way and that is the Ninth Amendment. This amendment reserves these rights to be defined by the individual, not by any form of government, federal or state. The only reason that federal and state officials do not want to give this right to the people is all about control. Government cannot stand to lose that control and therefore will blatantly disregard our individual right promised in the Ninth.

II. The Fourteenth Amendment, 1868

The Fourth, Fifth, and Sixth Amendments are integral rights to our persons' liberty protections. But not as the one that is important for us to define our rights within ourselves, the Ninth.

Roe's basis for its decision was founded on the Due Process Clause of the Fourteenth Amendment. The standing decision on *Casey* was like the one of *Roe*. They based it for federal government control to establish control upon the people of the various states. This right or power or whatever you want to call it, it does not belong to either form of governmental entity.

Why cannot people just understand that a federal or state government entity cannot rule on the morality issue towards its people.

The decision of abortion regrettably went back to the sovereign states to ponder that question and restrict the individual's liberty. The high court should have strongly considered to give this question to the individual, and not to any form of government. Also, the high court should finally have debunked this idea of substantive due process under the Fourteenth Amendment. Individuals already have rights, and do not need any higher right than the bill of rights. The issue of abortion has certainly reshaped our republic with an imaginary super right concocted to be added into the Fourteenth Amendment.

The rights of life, marriage, or use of their own private life is bestowed upon the individual. It is bestowed under that prized amendment before the states' amendment. The Fourteenth Amendment does not enter into any legal framework regarding on issue's pertaining to the livelihood of the private individual. It is a shame that even today, our government officials from federal to state to county to local authority fails to read our Constitution and comprehend our individual liberties under the bill of rights. In the issues of life, marriage on individuality... we need to reshape once again our republic, not reshape it in an odd fashion that in some cases of life, liberty, and the pursuit of happiness should not be denied and infringed or abridged.

F. Identity Relations

Any kind of identity, life, or marital relationship, or relationship issues, does not constitute for the government entity to define it and regulate it. Now comes to an overly critical issue that now involves the sense of individual sense of liberty towards an identity idea to be reshaped among our American republic of sovereign states. Among this issue as well as if it were a life or marriage issue belongs to the definition of the American individual. It is not best to be defined by a state government or the federal government entity.

Our status of our republic has been reshaping oddly because of the wrong interpretative words in defining the Fourteenth Amendment. These oddly interpretations of the Fourteenth Amendment based on these issues from both sides have caused a lot of headache and damage to our state of our republic.

Only once, a federal government official, member of the high court mentioned our most sacred right belonging to the Ninth Amendment of the Constitution. After that, the language of the Ninth Amendment has been likely to be stricken from our Constitution by both the left-wing progressives and right-wing nationalists.

Our individuals within our American republic of sovereign states have struggled in choosing to identify themselves. That

The Amendments

is the beauty of being an American representative republic of sovereign states. That this nation was built on the backbone of the individual self-reliance without the help, assistance, or dependency of a government entity.

I cannot and will speak about the sense of identity from other nations across this world. I will only speak for this republic's issues and the issue of our individual base are seeking to be identified to whatever they choose to be identified.

Even before this new identity situation started to enter our private and public eyes to our republic. The sense of identity for our individual Americans rely upon themselves and not within any government entity, federal or state government.

"In 2023, Tennessee joined the growing number of States restricting sex transition treatments for minors by enacting the Prohibition on Medical Procedures Performed on Minors Related to Sexual Identity, Senate Bill 1 (SB1). SB1 prohibits healthcare providers from prescribing, administering, or dispensing puberty blockers or hormones to any minor for the purpose of (1) enabling the minor to identify with, or live as, a purported identity inconsistent with the minor's biological sex, or (2) treating purported discomfort or distress from a discordance between the minor's biological sex and asserted identity. At the same time, SB1 permits a healthcare provider to administer puberty blockers or hormones to treat a minor's congenital defect, precocious puberty, disease, or physical injury." (Syllabus Brief of United States, Petitioner v. Jonathan Skrmetti, Attorney General and Reporter for Tennessee, 2025).

This is all about control, the government wants it. They want to remove it from the individuals. The government, whether federal or state governments have been doing it since the 1787 constitutional adoption. And you then look back and state, whatever happened to the individuality rights invoked in the "We the People" and the Ninth Amendment, right?

II. The Fourteenth Amendment, 1868

Tennessee and several other states signed a constitutional compact to enter this constitutional republic. Among this constitutional agreement was a little provision in the Bill of Rights known as the Ninth Amendment. Given that there are some powers not defined by either government, the powers to gain these rights are left for the individual to define and dictate.

"SB1 contains three primary enforcement mechanisms. The law authorizes Tennessee's attorney general to bring against any person who knowingly violates SB1 an action "to enjoin further violations, to disgorge any profits received to the medical procedure, and to recover a civil penalty of [$25,000] per violation." Section 68-33-106(b). SB1 further permits the relevant state regulatory authorities to discipline healthcare providers who violate the law's prohibitions. Section 68-33-107. Finally, SB1 creates a private right of action that enables an injured minor or nonconsenting parent of an injured minor to sue a healthcare provider for violating the law. Section 68-33-105." (Opinion Brief of United States, Petitioner v. Jonathan Skrmetti, Attorney General and Reporter for Tennessee, by Chief Justice John Roberts, 2025).

"The parties agree that the States have a legitimate interest in regulating healthcare." (Concurring Brief of United States, Petitioner v. Jonathan Skrmetti, Attorney General and Reporter for Tennessee, by Associate Justice Amy Coney Barrett, 2025).

The distinction between *de jure* discrimination and private animus is consistent with the Fourteenth Amendment's text and purpose. Most fundamentally, the Fourteenth Amendment constrains state action, not private conduct. Of course, this presumption can be defeated, and a widespread history of state action that reflects animus or stereotyping gives courts good reason to be suspicious of the government's motives. But because we presume that state actors abide by the Constitution, the fact of private discrimination—which is not itself unconstitutional, even if morally blameworthy—does not provide a basis for inferring that state actors are also likely to discriminate and thereby violate the Constitution." (Concurring Brief of United States, Petitioner v. Jonathan Skrmetti, Attorney General and Reporter for Tennessee, by Associate Justice Amy Coney Barrett, 2025).

The law in question from the Volunteer state, and other states, claims that prohibits "private" healthcare providers from instituting policies of transgender care towards its residents. The framers gave this power for the individual to manage his or her own life to their own accords. The genius behind the Ninth Amendment is for the individual to think for itself without any government assistance or dependency. Protection only enters the equation for justice. It does not mean to regulate that protection.

If people were to regulate for their own lives, we would not need any government assistance, dependency, or regulated protection. The regulatory statement from Justice Barrett and the plaintiffs is the reason the republic is in the mess that it is in with that sort of attitude. If we are expecting for the government, whether federal or state governments to come in and run our lives, then we can forfeit our Ninth Amendment right and live under an American Autocratic Democracy of dependent American states.

I want to inform my reader and my followers to really follow our Constitution's bill of rights and within these issues to invoke our Ninth Amendment right. To stop using the Fourteenth Amendment in oddly reshaping this American republic under false challenges on the Fourteenth Amendment.

"An estimated 1.6 million Americans over the age of 13 identify as transgender, meaning that their gender identity does not align with their biological sex." (Opinion Brief of United

II. The Fourteenth Amendment, 1868

States, Petitioner v. Jonathan Skrmetti, Attorney General and Reporter for Tennessee, by Chief Justice John Roberts, 2025).

"Three transgender minors, their parents, and a doctor (plaintiffs) brought a pre-enforcement challenge to SB1. Among other things, the plaintiffs asserted that SB1 violates the Equal Protection Clause of the Fourteenth Amendment." (Opinion Brief of United States, Petitioner v. Jonathan Skrmetti, Attorney General and Reporter for Tennessee, by Chief Justice John Roberts, 2025).

This was a grave and unconstitutional mistake on behalf of the plaintiffs and their parents. I shall explain below why it is a grave and unconstitutional mistake.

"The Court's willingness to do so here does irrevocable damage to the Equal Protection Clause and invites legislatures to engage in discrimination by hiding blatant sex classifications in plain sight." (Dissenting Brief of United States, Petitioner v. Jonathan Skrmetti, Attorney General and Reporter for Tennessee, by Associate Justice Sonia Sotomayor, 2025).

The ignorant politicians on both sides, parties, and movements, willingness has done more irrevocable damage to reshape the republic than any constitutional amendment. Legislatures across this republic of sovereign states will continue to engage in discrimination in plain sight hid to defend the individual's Ninth Amendment.

"The Fourteenth Amendment's command that no State shall "deny to any person within its jurisdiction to equal protection of the laws," U.S. Const., Amdt., 14, Section 1, "must coexist with the practical necessity that most legislation classifies for one purpose or another, with resulting disadvantage to various groups or persons," Romer v. Evans, 517 U.S. 620, 631, (1996)." (Opinion Brief of United States, Petitioner v. Jonathan Skrmetti, Attorney General and Reporter for Tennessee, by Chief Justice John Roberts, 2025).

The Amendments

This law and other laws like this one, whether federal or state, should have been deemed unconstitutional. It should have been deemed unconstitutional, not under a Fourteenth Amendment challenge, but a Ninth Amendment challenge.

"Transgender adolescents' access to hormones and puberty blockers (known as gender-affirming care) is not a matter of mere cosmetic preference. To the contrary, access to care can be a question of life or death. Some transgender adolescents suffer from gender dysphoria, a medical condition characterized by clinically significant and persistent distress resulting from incongruence between a person's gender identity and sex identified at birth." (Dissenting Brief of United States, Petitioner v. Jonathan Skrmetti, Attorney General and Reporter for Tennessee, by Associate Justice Sonia Sotomayor, 2025).

Medical defining terms should not be there to define simple constitutional terms. The individuality is the only one that should be allowed to dictate and define these terms based on the Constitution. To dictate and define and reshape it accordingly, not with a Fourteenth Amendment challenge but with a Ninth Amendment challenge.

"By retreating from meaningful judicial review exactly where it matters most, the Court abandons transgender children and their families to political whims. In sadness, I dissent." (Dissenting Brief of United States, Petitioner v. Jonathan Skrmetti, Attorney General and Reporter for Tennessee, by Associate Justice Sonia Sotomayor, 2025).

By retreating from meaningful judicial review exactly where it matters most, the Court, made up of right-wing nationalists and left-wing progressives abandons the heart of the American individual, regardless of an identity crisis to political whims. With great sadness, I dissent.

I am dissenting to the opinion of this court and to the dissenting opinions. I show no support for either side because both sides are against our Constitution. Both sides have not

II. The Fourteenth Amendment, 1868

read fully our principled document and these issues are not within a Fourteenth Amendment challenge, plain and simple.

* * *

Our motto for this republic, "All Equal Under Law." That motto stands tall among other nations and unique because we have that motto stamped with the sense of the pursuit of liberty, fraternity, and happiness. Thank god we live in this reshaped American republic of sovereign states. For the glory to have been reshaped for the better, and not for the worst.

III. The Fifteenth Amendment, 1870

Section I. The right of citizens of the United States to vote shall not be denied or abridged by the United States or by any State or by any State on account of race, color, or previous condition of servitude.

Section II. The Congress shall have power to enforce this article by appropriate legislation.

A. A Right to Vote for All

The right to vote has been granted by the federal government for all their individual citizens to share this right with equality. With equality when they go to cast their voting presence at the polling location. We would not be in this predicament if the General Government's high court would have not denied this authority and right to the sovereign states in the first place. But here we are, and we must now abide to what the national government failed to do prior to a bloody civil war conflict.

The federal government gives us this right and neither the national nor the individual state governments can deny us this right to vote. The right to vote and electoral voting standards are considered two different legal forms of electoral discussion in our republic. We are discussing the right to vote. The right to count these votes are delivered through the individual state legislatures.

We are talking about the establishment of this Fifteenth Amendment's right to vote and how it worked in this reshaped American republic of sovereign states.

If the repatriated southern rebellious states would just have continued to live their lives with just a little bit of a new change. We would not have had a meddling federal government. But we have had indeed a meddling national government on behalf of the troubled southern states, and we continue to have a meddling national government on the troubled behalf of various states. If the southern states and its individuals would have coexisted with the new American individuals that entered as people into our society, then we would not have had to amend the constitution to reshape this union. But we did and we are here to coexist and live together as Americans. Whether citizen or not, as American individuals.

The Fifteenth Amendment legislation was presented to the national house and a vote was held. The vote was one-hundred and forty-four to forty-four, with thirty-five members not voting. The members of the Democratic party voted against the legislation and joined by three Republican party members.

Unfortunately, the legislation did not consist of a protection to prohibit literacy tests or poll taxes and that is why the leading Republican abolitionist Charles Sumner voted against the measure. But the measure did pass both houses of the national Congress and sent for the several states to ratify the amendment.

Even though, the prohibition of poll taxes and literacy were not added to the Fifteenth Amendment, it was indeed covered in Section II of the Amendment. But again, unfortunately, the national Congress let the several states, predominately in the south to run wild. The national Congress denied to not fully enforce the Fifteenth Amendment's Section II to all its persons across their regions.

The congressional Enforcement Act of 1870 was a tool that was applied in due because of Section II. An official in the Commonwealth of Kentucky refused to register a black American's vote in a local election. The official was indicted under two sections of the 1870 act, section I, required that administrative preliminaries to elections be conducted without race, color, or previous condition of servitude; and

III. The Fifteenth Amendment, 1870

section II forbade wrongful refusal to register votes where a precondition step had been entered. The high court held in *United States v. Reese*, 1876, that the amendment did not confer the right of suffrage, but it prohibited the exclusion from voting on racial grounds. The majority stated that the section of the Enforcement Act of 1870 exceeded its authority of the Fifteenth Amendment.

Unfortunately, all these high court rulings came after the ill-fated massacre in Grant Parish, Colfax Louisiana. This was the first election in where black American individuals were granted the right to participate in the electoral process. Louisiana appeared to have a Republican party majority in both state houses and the governorship. But there were there some white individuals, former confederate soldiers, did not like the outcome of a Louisiana election. So, these white individuals gathered in the same area that the black individuals where and began pestering the newly freed and black citizens. Of course, violence broke out, probably from the white side first and all hell broke loose. Instead of the federal government set to defend these individuals with the guaranteed rights and protections of the Bill of Rights and Fourteenth Amendment affirmation, instead casted a blind eye. The high court and the Congress at that time decided not to grant any more leeway and protections, for whatever personal reason that they had in past experiences.

I also discuss another despicable and unconstitutional ruling in Chapter II, Race Relations, Page 38. This ruling was titled, *United States v. Cruikshank*, 1876. This ruling basically gave no second amendment rights and protections to these black American persons.

How come a congressional act is said to have exceeded its authority on the Fifteenth Amendment? Section II states that "Congress has the authority to present legislation to enforce

The Amendments

the said amendment." This was the beginning of unjust and unconstitutional enforcement of arrogant sovereign states accompanied with an arrogant General Government.

The Fifteenth Amendment's language is so clear to understand and to have the high court of the land found unconstitutional and unprincipled flaws is blatantly disgusting. Thus, began the era of several states denying the people's right to vote and the national high court affirming these decisions. Plus affirming the decisions of placing unjust poll taxation policies, thanks to the again affirmed Sixteenth Amendment.

The first, true Section II enforcement congressional legislation did not occur until 1890, presented by then-Representative Henry Cabot Lodge of Massachusetts. The Lodge bill of 1890, also known as the Federal Elections Bill/Lodge Force bill to propose to ensure a sense of security of elections for U.S. Representatives. But the fact of the matter was that the piece of legislation to enforce the ability of southern blacks, mostly republican at that time to vote in various southern states.

This bill was a true representation of the Fifteenth Amendment's section II and Henry Cabot Lodge was a true constitutionalist. But alas, the national Congress had a quite a few racist legislators, from both parties that denied this bill to go through. It barely passed the national house of representatives by a merely six votes but was unsuccessful in the national senate. Mostly southern Democrats filibustered the bill and decided to trade in this vote for a republican-supported tariff act. Typical from Washington City politicians, betraying a true constitutional principle over a false one. The right of voting protections over a federal direct tax…a quite common thing occurring and still occurring in our nation's capital.

III. The Fifteenth Amendment, 1870

The Lodge bill was the first in its finest and truest moments of constitutionality that began to reshape this republic. But, unfortunately, this bill which was a stepping-stone to bring forth a reshaping equality to our American republic led us to more troubling times.

As we saw various members of the national Congress and even our high court jurists deny equal protection of the law to our newly made individuals feel unwelcome into our republic. The federal national Congress passed an amendment and then ratified by the various states. The amendment was to give the right to vote for all Americans regardless of race, or color. Yet, we have seen various states and even the high court deny this right on all fronts.

In 1903, the high court continued to deny the rights of all citizens based on its right to vote. The holding of this decision should have shared some light to our nation's Congress to bring in some defense towards these individuals.

"The Court refused to assist African Americans in Alabama who were systematically denied the right to vote by a scheme set up by the all-white state legislature." (Opinion Brief of Giles v. Harris, by Associate Justice Oliver Wendell Holmes, 1903).

It is not the duty of the Court to offer and give assistance and protection to an American individual. It is strictly written in the Fifteenth Amendment that it is within the duty of the Congress to enforce this amendment with the adequate legislation to defend the guaranteed rights and protections for all Americans.

"First, the Court noted the plaintiffs were asserting that the entire registration system was unconstitutional, but the only relief they sought was to be registered. The Court suggested that it could not order the names of the plaintiffs to be added to the voter rolls, while the entire voting process remained illegal, since doing so would make the court complicit in an illegal scheme." (Opinion Brief of Giles v. Harris, by Associate Justice Oliver Wendell Holmes, 1903).

Justice John Marshall Harlan, along with Justice David Josiah Brewer dissented on this decision. They both claimed that the court system could had the absolute answer to this question to have it resolved by the courts. I would agree and disagree with the assessments of both justices. The court system is there to find injustices in the laws enacted by the national Congress and individual state legislatures. It is their duty to advise the legislative aspect of the government, whether national or state to revise, amend, or repeal the laws. To accommodate all the citizens affected by an unjust law.

The aftermath of several black American individuals obtained the right to vote continued to receive backlash, racist discrimination, and most importantly the denial of their right to vote. The plaintiff Jackson W. Giles, after he was denied justice from this case. He continued to fight for the electoral voting right cause for him and for individuals like him that had been denied the right to vote.

This case just happened to be in Alabama, but the sad truth is that it was being effected across the several states, not only in the south. But the fight was indeed in most of the southern states, not just in Alabama, but in Mississippi, Georgia, South Carolina, Florida, etc.

Like the high court found residential segregation to be unconstitutional in 1917 under the Fourteenth Amendment. The high court found the several grandfathered clauses of the type of state's voting systems to be unconstitutional. Yet, the various several states continue to ignore the will of the constitutional opinion of the court system and decide to ignore the Constitution's newly reshaped amendments.

As I continue to remind people across this republic. We would not have had such an overstepped federal government

III. The Fifteenth Amendment, 1870

in these voting policies if politicians and people read the Constitution more clearly and its constitutional-appropriate rulings along with them.

In 1915, the Supreme Court of the United States decided on *Guinn v. United States*, to begin to dismantle, but not annihilate the white-only primary systems across the southern states. But what they did was a stepping ground into the right direction. The court declared that the grandfathered clauses of various states' electoral codes in putting a barrier between the minority-voter and its ballot box was an infringement on their Fifteenth Amendment's right. This case also dismantled the form of literacy tests in obtaining a ballot.

All unconstitutional disorder either begins in the Lone Star state or the Magnolia state. But this time it began in the state of Oklahoma.

The right to vote has been infringed for such a long time as various southern states enacted these grandfathered clauses into their electoral laws and codes. The grandfathered clauses may have been eliminated as a disenfranchisement towards various voters based on their race or color. But the systematic violation of the Fifteenth Amendment continued to rein in as various southern states continued to pursue white-only policies under their Democratic party, the party of a failed Confederate government but always relying for privilege for them and denying it to others. Now we see party politics shift towards the Republican party.

When a constitutional opinion of the high court raises no dissenting opinion, and the opinion is constitutionally biased...then it must be unconstitutionally biased.

After we have seen the high court state an opinion dismantling the ill-will of literacy tests, a state continued to adopt similar state directives that once again violated the very presence of the Fifteenth Amendment.

The Amendments

The various several in the south and western states were the culprits in denying the right to vote towards these American individuals based on the race and color. It is a definite violation of their equal rights under the Fourteenth, but the Fifteenth Amendment is clear in its language.

Sometimes we need the courts to adopt appropriate constitutional measures to ensure that the constitution is served and adopted. In *Lane v. Wilson*, 1939, the high court the power of county registrars from illegally excluding black citizens from the voting polls. And yet, this ruling was made in 1939 and somehow county registrars with the support of state government executives allowed them to continuously contradict this ruling and the Fifteenth Amendment.

If people of all color would have read supreme court rulings and even the constitution, we would not have had a bloody Sunday in Selma, Alabama.

The party of the old South was the Democratic party. This party was once the denier of voting rights for all American individuals but extending to some. Now unfortunately, it has become the Republican party, the old once-Democratic party. The old, infamous two-party switch of 1964.

How about to have a two or three or multiple political party system that obeys and maintains the Constitution as fully written.

The Democratic party of Texas adopted a plan to ban black-voting residents in primary elections within the state of Texas. Of course, the lower courts stood with bigotry and hatred towards these individuals. This individual R.R. Grovey, a black Texan resident took his case all the way to the high court.

Deeply unfortunately, the Supreme Court still had unwise jurists like when they had back in 1857. They ruled a political party as a private organization and not fit to be equal under

III. The Fifteenth Amendment, 1870

law for all in *Grovey v. Townsend*, 1935. Interesting, two of the most progressive jurists of this court, Justices Louis Brandeis and Benjamin Cardozo would align themselves in electoral bigotry and not with the Fifteenth Amendment. Not surprising because progressive critics or nationalist skeptics will typically side with prejudice special interests and not align with constitutional interests.

It will take a brand-new court membership to realize the constitutional threat among all our American individuals that wish to participate in our elections. In an eight to one court decision in 1944, it was decided that denying a person of color to participate in an election, whether in a primary or general election. It was a definite violation of its Fifteenth Amendment promise to the voter.

Tragically and regrettably, there was a lone unconstitutional dissenter that Justice Marshall Harlan would haunt his opinion to the grave. Associate Justice Owen Roberts, appointed by President Herbert Hoover sided with electoral bigotry over the constitution. He dissents that these elections are run by a certain party and not by the state or federal governments. And I rebuff to that statement by saying that if a state or party wishes to receive federal funds, then they are not only obliged to obey the Constitution, even if they receive or not receive federal funds. In my opinion, private companies, and private universities, in which they receive their share of federal and/or state government dependent dollars. They lose all their credibility and exemption in being a private entity.

This was a great step for ending voter intimidation and discrimination at the ballot box in not only in Texas, but all across our states. But, unfortunately, still the bigoted individuals were still a problem in our union and still were denying people's the proper participation into our American voting process.

The Amendments

Neither the federal government nor an individual sovereign state shall infringe upon its American individual's right to vote. But sadly, the abuse continued, and the federal national Congress did nothing to accommodate a Section V enforcement of the Fifteenth Amendment. The abuse ended in 1965 with the passage of the Voting Rights Act.

B. The Right to Vote of 1965

Because the voting infringement continued throughout the middle of the twentieth century. Neither the state governments in those rebellious states, or the federal government ever sided with the affected voter and enforced the rightful amendment with the appropriate legislation.

The federal government tackled the civil rights issue with multiple legislation. But not one of those congressional acts consisted of the guaranteed protection of the Fifteenth Amendment. That scene changed when national media outlets and all around the nation witnessed the terrible ordeal that occurred in Selma, Alabama, 1965. Quite sadly, it took one day to spark an outrage in Congress to pass the Voting Rights Act of 1965, after several hundreds of years before then, and nobody did anything to stop it.

On August 6, 1965, the 1965 Voting Rights Act was signed into law by President Lyndon B. Johnson. This act in theory affirmed the Fifteenth Amendment in its guaranteed voting right promise. But in future years, we would see future jurists, politicians, and media pundits begin to undermine the role of the sovereign state and introduce a distorted wave of centralized electoral autonomy.

The Amendments

"An Act to enforce the Fifteenth Amendment of the Constitution of the United States, and for other purposes."
Section II: No voting qualification or prerequisite to voting, or standard practice, or procedure shall be imposed or applied by any State or political subdivision to deny or abridge the right of any citizen of the United States to vote on account of race or color.
Section III (a): Whenever the Attorney General institutes a proceeding under any statute to enforce the guarantees of the Fifteenth Amendment in any State or political subdivision. The court shall authorize the appointment of Federal examiners by the United States Civil Service Commission in accordance to section six to serve for such period of time and for such political subdivisions as the court shall determine is appropriate to enforce the guarantees of the Fifteenth Amendment.

I am not THAT person in for denying the voting right of the individual. But I am also not THAT person in denying the electoral right of a sovereign state. As we all know through history, if the sovereign states knew how to play the rules of American federalism. We would not be in this predicament of federalizing our Electoral Clauses, by mere attacks of political partisanship. But we are in this predicament and we need to adjust and reshape this republic to preserve our sense of liberty and equality.

The sovereign states prior to 1965 used their bigoted might to enforce unjust electoral laws and standards against all our individuals of our union within their state. These

III. The Fifteenth Amendment, 1870

laws consisted of excessive literacy tests that withheld the citizen from entering the voting booth. Also consisted of excessive taxes known as poll taxes from a registration tax to allowing them to enter the voting booth. These laws were extremely targeted for not only voter suppression. But also, voter infringement upon a Fifteenth Amendment violation.

The Voting Rights Act of 1965 was the first and mostly the only actual appropriate legislation by Congress to protect the integrity of the Fifteenth Amendment. For years and centuries, it took the national Congress to finally secure the appropriate legislation to enforce this amendment. But, alas, as there were individuals seeking to undermine the role of the sovereign state within the Fourteenth Amendment. They have been and still are individuals from all sides of the political spectrum trying to undermine the actual role of this amendment and the sovereign states.

The act states that it is up to the Attorney General of the United States to initiate any action against any state conducting any voting intimidation or violations against a voter of their state. Yes, sometimes there will be injustices, but the injustices must be filed in accordance with the law. Congress gave this authority to this department of the federal executive branch. As the constitutional framers gave the appropriate wisdom of its heirs to constitute appropriately the Constitution. So does the heirs of the authors of the Fifteenth Amendment.

Like I said before, there were individuals trying to undermine not only the guaranteed right of this amendment. But undermining the role of each sovereign state's electoral right under the electoral clauses.

Right-wing nationalist skeptics or left-wing progressive critics will try to undermine one or both areas that pertain to the elections of a state. Whether they will undermine the meaning of the electoral clauses, or the Fifteenth Amendment. Federal legislators have tried in the past and continue to try to undermine the Fifteenth Amendment and along the electoral clauses to state their own electoral standard of a nationalistic bigoted special interest. They have tried, not quite with federal legislation, but in various state legislatures to advance political partisan electoral measures. By advancing in a way to deny individual's right to vote by adding electoral unnecessary extremities. It is not the same as poll taxes, or literacy tests. But it can be construed to be identified as voting restrictions, *Mark Brnovivh, Attorney General of Arizona, Et Al., Petitioners v. Democratic National Committee, Et Al.* I will be discussing down the line the issue that is happening and has been happening across our union. Gerrymandering, a tool for principled voting and not political partisan voting.

* * *

Because of the various southern states that have denied their citizens' right to vote in various elections. The federal Congress has stepped with federal enforcement as instructed in section V of the Fifteenth Amendment. The appropriate legislative enforcement was inducted in 1965 with the Voting Rights Act. The purpose of this act is strictly to authorize the federal government any abuses by any city, county, or state electoral official denying a person's right to vote based on his race or color.

Because of long-standing abuse by various states, the federal Congress, the high court feels that there is continued abuses and discourages of minority-based voters.

I believe in the independent state legislature theory, which is very must a reality. A reality bestowed by our constitutional framers for our individual states to enforce

III. The Fifteenth Amendment, 1870

and control our elections. But in recent times, the framers of the Fifteenth Amendment bestowed upon us the right to vote for all citizens.

But because of the current federal government enforcement of the Fifteenth Amendment with the 1965 Voting Rights Act, the political party system has been a complete disregard of this amendment and our electoral clauses.

The Voting Rights Act of 1965 started out to be a good cause to be a federal legislative enforcement tool for the Fifteenth Amendment. As time progressed and less abuses of voter right infringement became more extinct. Both sides of this annoying two-political party system began to search ways to abuse their power. By abusing the main role of the 1965 act and undermine the true purpose of this amendment to coincide them together in federalism and racial equality with liberty.

* * *

There has been many high court rulings and federal executive legal precedents undermining the role of the citizen's right to vote role within our state elections and against the electoral clauses state's sovereign right. The electoral clauses should not come into play while defining the role of the Fifteenth Amendment. In my humble constitutional opinion, it has two different purposes in our constitutional way of life.

For the question to state that the state courts are here to dictate what rules are deemed appropriate to ensure a "fair" and "free" election, is a power that the Courts do not have and never had. The courts are not here to determine the rules. The courts are here to interpret the rules and if they deemed it unconstitutional. Their job is to not strike a law, but advise the legislature thereof, to amend and/or repeal the rules. "The executive of the State is there to execute the

The Amendments

law, or veto the law, if the governor does not see fit that this law is constitutionally viable." (*Smiley v. Horn*, 1932).

And here we go on the ride to see who will dictate electoral standards for our republic. Here we go again, to see how the federal government with its left-wing progressive critics and right-wing nationalist skeptics continue to undermine our Fifteenth Amendment and electoral clauses. By trying to forcibly join them or unjoin them and creating a mess of things to damage our fragile constitutional American republic.

The Fifteenth Amendment was established for all our citizens, the guaranteed right to vote. It is the right to request an electoral ballot without any hassle of harassment or intimidation. What the Fifteenth Amendment does not say is that the federal government, the right to impose national electoral and counting standards. The 1965 Voting Rights Act affirmed the guaranteed right to vote, it does not affirm a counting standard. That counting standard is being left to the sovereign States to regulate and enforce. It is that quite simple, and we all know why the general government wants to bypass the states' authority… it is all about control.

When I state that the power is reserved to the sovereign States, it is clearly meant by the state legislature. The state legislature is the directive's voice of and for the people.

"Were they exclusively under the control of the state governments, the general government might be easily dissolved. But if they be regulated properly by the state legislatures, the congressional control will very probably never be exercised."
(The Debates in the Several States Conventions, vol. 3, James Madison).

Even before, the sound of equal liberty bells rang within our republic, Madison understood the electoral legal frameworks for our republic. The Fifteenth Amendment added a sense of equal liberty in the voting booths.

III. The Fifteenth Amendment, 1870

Only a few jurists of the court have interpreted the constitution author's words onto theirs and kept it in the original format as presented to the convention in 1787. The late Associate Justice to the high court, Justice Antonin Scalia truly was the sole jurist that spoke the wordings of the Constitution as they were written on it. He made no mistakes in expressing his original intent views and never presented the principled document as a "living-Original" document. The Constitution is an original document residing in a world of today living up to its principled standards. The electoral clauses in the Constitution resides in the power of the States and not the national government. The enforcement right to protect the citizen's right to vote resides within the federal government, not the states. But they must coincide together to be able to survive within our federalism American republic of sovereign states.

"It seems to me utterly implausible that the Framers wanted federal courts limited to traditional judicial cases only when they were pronouncing upon the rights of Congress and the President, and not when they were treading upon the powers of state legislatures and executives. Quite to the contrary, I think they would be *all the more averse* to unprecedented judicial meddling by federal courts with the branches of their state governments." (Dissenting Opinion of Arizona State Legislature v. Arizona Independent Redistricting Commission, by Associate Justice Antonin Scalia, 2015).

Justice Scalia knew what court cases and legislation belongs in the hands of the federal government and the sovereign states. Electoral laws and standards, from national presidential elections to statewide elections belongs in the hands of the state legislatures. The federal government granted this right for all sovereign States to give their citizens, the right to vote. But the federal government was not granted the right, nor the power to control the electoral counting and standards of each state's elections.

"Normally, having arrived at that conclusion, I would express no opinion on the merits unless my vote was necessary to enable the court to product a judgment. In the present case, however, the majority's resolution of merits question ("legislature means "the people") is so outrageously wrong, so utterly devoid of textual or historic support, so flatly in contradiction of prior Supreme Court cases, so obviously the willful product of hostility to districting by state legislatures, that I cannot adding my vote to the devastating dissent of the Chief Justice." (Dissenting Opinion of Arizona State Legislature v. Arizona Independent Redistricting Commission, by Associate Justice Antonin Scalia, 2015).

Districting and re-districting of electoral areas in a sovereign State belongs in the realm of law to the sovereign State. The state legislature is not denying that person's right to vote, just because they re-district that voting location. It is a standard of electoral law and that still resides under Constitutional Article II.

This is where the ignorance and arrogance of this political party system comes to play trying to undermine our amendment's right to vote and our electoral clauses. When you undermine the Constitution, whether the electoral clauses or the Fifteenth Amendment. You undermine and bring confusion to the basic language of these items to our federal constitution.

"Second, after the Constitution was ratified, states kept regulating it. States like Delaware and Maryland and Mississippi expressly regulated federal elections, as did three quarters of the states." (Oral Argument of Mr. Neal K. Katyal, on behalf of the respondents on Moore v. Harper, December 7, 2022).

One thing is to deny a constitutional right to vote, and the other is to regulate elections. A state can continue to regulate

III. The Fifteenth Amendment, 1870

elections without infringing on that constitutional right to vote. In all the electoral standards and laws that came after *Bush v. Gore*, 2000. I truly see no voter rights infringement of the citizens' Fifteenth Amendment voting right.

To this day, since after 1965, no sovereign State has yet denied the right to vote to an American individual. The Fifteenth Amendment has guaranteed that right since 1868. Then it was re-affirmed with the passage of the Voting Rights Act (VRA) in 1965. What the VRA does not state or make claim of is that it does not grant the federal government to create and mandate a national standard of voting.

"So the State has no duty to substitute a non-discriminatory rule that would adequately serve its professed goal. Like the rest of today's opinion, the majority's treatment of the collection ban flouts what Section 2 commands: the eradication of election rules resulting in unequal opportunities for minority voters." (Dissenting Opinion on Mark Brnovivh, Attorney General of Arizona, Et Al., Petitioners v. Democratic National Committee, Et Al. by Associate Justice Elena Kagan, 2021).

Removing drop ballots boxes or directing voters to their proper polling place is not a new result of showing unequal opportunities to any such voter. This is not 1957 Alabama where poll taxes and literacy tests were a classic move of voter suppression and denying our basic Fifteenth Amendment right to vote. The Voting Rights Act of 1965 says it in its name. It is the Right to Vote Act, not the Counting Votes Act.

The Arizona electoral law in question has flaws that nobody dares to bring up. They are putting more ballot boxes on the streets but redistricting the polling places across the state. The voting standards and counting procedures should be equal at best and not so a

> It is the Right to Vote Act, not the Counting Votes Act.

The Amendments

disproportionate in showing access in one way and diminish access to the other. As long as electoral officials of any state are not denying the right to vote of that individual, then there should not be any lawsuits filed as a challenge to the Fifteenth Amendment.

"But Congress gets to make that call. Because it has not done so, this Court's duty is to apply the law as it is written. The law that confronted one of this country's most enduring wrongs; pledged to give every American, of every race, an equal chance to participate in our democracy; and now stands as the crucial tool to achieve that goal. That law, of all laws, deserves the sweep and power Congress gave it. That law, of all laws, should not be diminished by this Court." (Dissenting Opinion on Mark Brnovivh, Attorney General of Arizona, Et Al., Petitioners v. Democratic National Committee, Et Al. by Associate Justice Elena Kagan, 2021).

Indeed, that the national Congress made that call. They made it so that everybody has the right to vote and equal access to an individual ballot. And in 1965, they affirmed that directive. But the Congress did not affirm anything to have a national counting directive for all the sovereign states. And the Court is to interpret a state or federal law, not to amend or repeal it.

If the Fifteenth Amendment becomes diminished by any governing body of the general government or individual sovereign state. Then the citizen has a right to complain, till then, the right to vote has not been diminished.

"Arizona's out-of-precinct policy and HB 2023 do not violate Section 2 of the VRA, and HB2023 was not enacted with a racially discriminatory purpose. The judgement of the Court of Appeals is reversed, and the cases are remanded for further proceedings consistent with this opinion. It is so ordered." (Opinion Brief on Mark Brnovivh, Attorney General of Arizona, Et

III. The Fifteenth Amendment, 1870

Al., Petitioners v. Democratic National Committee, Et Al. by Associate Justice Samuel Alito, 2021).

The sovereign states understand that after 1965, the right to vote should not be denied to all citizens of this republic. The Voting Rights Act shows affirmation of the Fifteenth Amendment that no vote shall be violated or prohibit to be casted. The votes are being casted, now comes that the voter should comprehend the standard and procedure of their state electoral laws.

As Justice Sandra Day O'Connor once stated in the 2000 case of *Bush v. Gore* towards the voter's participation in their right to vote.

"Why is not it the standard, the one that voters are instructed to follow, for goodness sake, I mean it could not be clearer. Why don't we go to that standard?" – Associate Justice Sandra Day O'Connor, *Bush v. Gore*, 2000.

The voters have a right to vote, and with that right to vote comes responsibility and understanding to follow it, to continue to obtain that right.

* * *

The federal government, whether the federal executive branch, national Congress or high court has truly been trying to undermine our constitutional electoral principles established in 1787 and amended in 1870.

This form of educative electoral agency is nothing more than infiltrating and undermining the rightly state sovereign doctrine articles that states have received since 1787, amended in 1870, and affirmed in 1965.

"While vote by mail appears to increase turnout for local elections, there is no evidence that it significantly expands participation in federal elections. Moreover, it raises concerns about privacy, as citizens voting at home may come under

The Amendments

pressure to vote for certain candidates, and it increases the risk of fraud. Oregon appears to have avoided significant fraud in its vote-by-mail elections by introducing safeguards to protect ballot integrity, including signature verification. Vote by mail is, however, likely to increase the risks of fraud and of contested elections in other states, where the population is more mobile, where there is some history of troubled elections, or where the safeguards for ballot integrity are weaker. (Report of the Comm'n on Fed. Election Reform, Building Confidence in U.S. Elections 46 (Sept. 2005).

"The case of King County, Washington, is instructive. In the 2004 gubernatorial elections, when two in three ballots there were cast by mail, authorities lacked an effective system to track the number of ballots sent or returned. As a result, King County election officials were unable to account for all absentee ballots. Moreover, a number of provisional ballots were accepted without signature verification. The failures to account for all absentee ballots and to verify signatures on provisional ballots became issues in the protracted litigation that followed Washington state's 2004 gubernatorial election." (Report of the Comm'n on Fed. Election Reform, Building Confidence in U.S. Elections 46 (Sept. 2005).

My concern to this Arizona electoral law is not the idea of vote-by-mail as I see it. It is the constant contradiction of the legal perks of vote-by-mail and the vote-in-person. Arizona's HB2023 gives electoral leeway to the voter by sending off their ballot in many different forms. The issue I have is that when you give too much leeway to one form of voting but not to the other is a recipe for misleading and legal turmoil. In this vote-by-mail to what Arizona is offering to her citizens is wide range of sending off their ballots in different formats. While if you vote-in-person, you are required to go to the assigned specific location and

III. The Fifteenth Amendment, 1870

if arrived at another polling place, you are being directed to the assigned one. If in person, you are being directed to your assigned voting location, why can't your ballot?

A state is not denying the citizen's right to vote. It is making the citizen scramble to go cast their vote all over the state of Arizona while giving easier access to absentee ballots. I do not see this as voter infringement or denial, just annoyance and confusion. An annoyance and confusion concocted by state legislators, being a state issue, not a federal issue.

If the sovereign state of Oregon has created a system that shows no signs of corruption or discriminatory intent. Then other states should follow that example and apply a similar standard but under their own law and regulations. If Oregon requires a "signature verification" on their absentee ballot, and is a must, then there are no exemptions to the rule and voters are expected to follow that rule. That rule of federalism.

If there is a state government employee not following that rule and finds a way to commit a corrupt act or discriminatory intent. That government employee must be investigated, and if proved of their guilty changes, must be prosecuted, and sentenced. If in Washington State, they also required a signature verification on their ballots and some were not verified, then there is a state government employee taking the rule into their own hands and must be dealt properly in the due process system established in this republic.

It is the solemn duty of a sovereign state to regulate and enforce the election rule. It is not intended for the states to diminish the right to vote of a citizen.

To handle acts of corruption and findings of discriminatory intent in elections are best handled by the sovereign state.

The Amendments

It is the solemn duty of the sovereign state to regulate and enforce that election rule. It is not intended for the national government to regulate elections.

I see there is a problem with the electoral law of the sovereign state of Washington. Sovereign states can follow other states' models of electoral law if it is applied at their own legislative procedure. We cannot let the courts apply without legislative affirmation. As we saw the debacle in Florida, 2000, and the constant harassment in 2020 and in our latest election in 2024.

The Carter-Baker Electoral Commission Report was presented to the republic as a notice to all sovereign states to apply the Constitution as it is currently written into their laws. They are simply recommending to the sovereign states. When the federal government, whether it is the high court, national Congress, or the executive branch tries to recommend any actions to the states, it leads to further control of the sovereignty of the states. One of them is the strict assurance that their residents of their state are confined to vote without no hint of harassment or discrimination. After 1965, with the national congressional assistance to enforce the Fifteenth Amendment, sovereign states have been given strict instructions to comply. Till this day, we have not seen any more days of Jim Crow laws in southern and rocky mountain states.

From what I have read, this report is not stating, and hope does not state on other parts, the consideration of a national electoral law. This is something that I do hope it never comes to existence because that will *truly* be the end of our American Republic of sovereign States.

The Fifteenth Amendment is the strict assurance guaranteed right of the citizen's right to vote. When state legislatures or national Congress play politics to undermine this citizen

III. The Fifteenth Amendment, 1870

right or state electoral right. It downplays our American republic's existence of liberty and equality as promised by our original framers to the amendment framers of the civil war amendments. That both coincide together for us to pursue a life of liberty and happiness for all to endure.

A national electoral law will inherently damage our citizen's right to vote by undermining our right within the Constitution. But, ultimately it will damage and cripple our electoral clauses.

C. Gerrymandering: A tool of Principled Voting

Gerrymandering is an electoral tool not to play politics with. It is a tool to help sway different principled ideas throughout a district's political ideas to benefit a sovereign state, not a nation or its federal government. Elbridge Gerry, a constitutional framer that was named after this electoral tool known as gerrymandering. He was not a man of partisan politics, but of principled politics. The principled political ideas of Elbridge Gerry have been moved away into a more political partisan thought process. From both sides of the political party spectrum, they have been playing politics and ruining the scrutiny of this electoral tool.

They have attacked the idea of gerrymandering into a partisan issue. Gerrymandering is a tool to enhance voter participation for new ideas, not a sense of voter suppression by partisan means. Both sides have lost the meaning of gerrymandering. They lost the meaning of the Electoral Clauses of the Constitution and the newly added Fifteenth Amendment.

We are now seeing new divisions in every single election and before every single election. Various constitutional framers saw the dangers of a political party system, especially a two-party system. In my constitutional opinion, this gerrymandering process works better with a multi-party system. A multi-party system has different shared one-thousand ideas

III. The Fifteenth Amendment, 1870

instead of two ideas. With this now two-party system, they have concocted wordings like "red states" v. "blue states" and created unnecessary divisions for our American union of sovereign states.

Red states belonging to one party, the Republican party. Blue states belonging to another party, the Democratic party. Different ideas should not be concocted to a party. Different ideas should be concocted from individual citizen ideas uniting in to one common constitutional cause. Political parties have corrupted our American republic slowly into an American dictatorship. Political parties have done nothing but damage the integrity and principles of our union of sovereign states. Political parties have manipulated to undermine the federal government's power of the Fifteenth Amendment is absolutely disgusting as well as our Electoral Clauses. But the most disgusting thing is the way they use the form of gerrymandering tool to undermine this amendment in the name of the electoral clauses.

Because of these shady tactics used in the name for gerrymandering that political parties are using. They are destroying the electoral clauses of the Constitution, but also destroying the sanctity of the right to vote that the Fifteenth Amendment promises all its citizens.

The Voting Rights Act of 1965 is an enforcement tool for the national Congress to enforce the right to vote for all citizens of this republic. It is with accordance to the guaranteed constitutional right of the Fifteenth Amendment. But while the American citizens have this right to vote, the states have theirs guaranteed with the electoral clauses.

But unfortunately, as a disgusting display of partisan politics have entered into a vulgar display of electoral discussions in these current years of our American republic. We have seen contradictory policies towards our Constitution.

The Amendments

Whether it is an attack on our Electoral Clauses or the Fifteenth Amendment. Most recently, in 2023, we saw one political party introduced The John Lewis Voting Rights Advancement Act by national house representative Terri Sewell of Alabama. Then in 2025, we see the introduction of The Making American Elections Great Again Act by national house of representative Marjorie Taylor Greene of Georgia. Both acts are a disgrace to our Constitution. Both speak unconstitutional volumes of democratic values, which our union of sovereign states is a representative republic form of government. Our union is not a united democracy, regardless to what modern politicians and media pundits acknowledge it to be.

You would imagine that our nation and its people would have learned of our 2000 election debacle. But, alas, no, after this debacle that we had to unconstitutionally had to use the judicial system into our electoral clauses, we are paying this ignorant price of not reading our principled document.

The Supreme Court has not yet defined this clause as a federal government enforcement tool. The national Congress, from either majority political party has tried, but so far has failed. The federal executive branch, from both political parties have also tried to achieve but failed. When will the federal government political and bureaucratic world of Washington City realize to read the Fifteenth Amendment and the Electoral Clauses? The two rights are separate from one another but must co-exist together in order to form a glorious American republic of sovereign states. The role of gerrymandering only comes to play nowadays to be able to define the role of the Fifteenth to coexist with the clauses. But the evil of this political party system has clouded the constitutional judgment to govern well among this republic.

III. The Fifteenth Amendment, 1870

The only reason this political party system divides and conquers into congressional districts is to achieve power and control. Neither the Republican or Democratic party cares for the individual's right to vote, let alone the electoral clauses.

There have been multiple examples of this two-party system use the state legislature of their state to enact electoral laws to divide and conquer on their congressional districts. Both parties in recent years and now currently have disavowed our state's sovereign right of the Electoral Clauses and its citizen's right to vote.

I pointed out in this chapter, a disgusting form of controlling a state's own electoral laws and standards in the Supreme Court case of *Mark Brnovivh, Attorney General of Arizona, Et Al., Petitioners v. Democratic National Committee, Et Al.*, and its aspect on that Arizona state electoral law. This Arizona law was extremely contradictory to not only our electoral clauses but to the Fifteenth Amendment.

Enter the current Vice-President of the United States JD Vance:

The current Vice-President, JD Vance said recently in a quote, "The gerrymander in California is outrageous. Of their 52 congressional districts, 9 of them are Republican. That means 17 percent of their delegation is Republican when Republicans regularly win 40 percent of the vote in that state. How can this possibly be allowed?" I feel pity for the office of the Vice-President of the United States. It is an office of no importance whatsoever and uselessness. Therefore, every time this bureaucrat opens his mouth… it is to spew nonsense and incoherent unconstitutional nonsense.

The way, I sadly see the California electoral map is just the way I see the North Carolina map. It is how the political party structure is being built within each state legislature.

The Amendments

Now it is the duty of any political party structure to maintain its constitutional structure over any political party structure.

Enter *Moore v. Harper* of 2023:
The independent state legislature theory is not a theory of partisan politics. It is very much a reality of principled politics. Despite what the federal high court decrees. The independence of the state legislature in the case of electoral laws lies within the independence of Article II. The amendment process, in this case with the Fifteenth Amendment, does not change the role of the independence and individual state assembly.

States just have to respect the will of this amendment, and the will to the right to vote. But unfortunately, with the introduction of this amendment, various state assemblies began to discard the citizen's right to vote by various forms of legislations against this amendment and the only enacted enforcement law laid down by the national government.

As I stated before, there is no beyond legal and constitutional reason, the electoral clauses to clash with the Fifteenth Amendment.

The Elections Clause of the Federal Constitution requires "the Legislature" of each State to prescribe the rules governing federal elections. Art. I, Section 4, cl. 4." (Judgment syllabus of Moore v. Harper, 2023).

"This Court has jurisdiction to review the judgement of the North Carolina Supreme Court in Harper I that adjudicated the Federal Elections Clause." (Judgment syllabus of Moore v. Harper, 2023).

Drawing congressional maps, executing voting standards and procedures are all legal processes set by Article I, II and under its Tenth Amendment doctrine. This should not have a negative effect on the citizen's right to vote as guaranteed in its Fifteenth Amendment.

III. The Fifteenth Amendment, 1870

"JUSTICE THOMAS sees it differently. He correctly observes that the North Carolina Supreme Court has now dismissed the plaintiffs' claims with prejudice." (Opinion of the Court for Moore v. Harper, 2023 by Chief Justice John Roberts).

The North Carolina legislature, being made up of mostly of one political party, decided to play party politics and not principled politics. The way many state legislatures have found ways to redistrict their state to have that political party to control, not only that state, but the national government.

"We conclude that partisan gerrymandering claims present political questions beyond the reach of the federal courts." (Opinion Brief by Chief Justice John Roberts for Rucho v. Common Cause, 2019).

It may be out of reach of federal courts, but according to the high court, not to the reaches of the state's supreme court. That is what the high court of the land did in 2024 with the decision of *Moore v. Harper*, and the one that sealed the fate for the win of Trump-Vance presidential campaign in 2024. But the even thought to present to any state legislature, a legislation for "partisan gerrymandering" goes against the very principle of the tool of gerrymandering. It goes against to the very heart of the constitution, from the Electoral Clauses to the Fifteenth Amendment.

"As a result, racial gerrymandering and vote dilution claims brought under the Fourteenth and Fifteenth Amendments are nonjusticiable." (Concurring Opinion by Associate Justice C. Thomas for Alexander, President of the South Carolina Senate v. South Carolina State Conference of the NAACP, 2024).

Determining how a legislature would have drawn district lines in a vacuum is a fool's errand." (Concurring Opinion by Associate Justice C. Thomas for Alexander, President of the South Carolina Senate v. South Carolina State Conference of the NAACP, 2024).

Partisan gerrymandering can be construed to racial gerrymandering. In the years after the Fifteenth Amendment's

The Amendments

adoption, a (Democratic) party that controlled the various southern state legislatures were establishing extreme racial electoral laws that included racist partisan gerrymandering. Plus, even denying the right to vote to their citizens, a clear violation of this amendment.

Nowadays, these same state legislatures, a new political (Republican) party controls them and have enacted partisan gerrymandering, but not to the extreme in denying their citizens' right to vote. There has been no strict evidence of discriminatory intent yet presented in any case.

In Arizona, the electoral law being disputed was not a discriminatory intent case, it was a misguided one. Arizona legislators presented a strange way to collect and count their ballots, but there was no racial gerrymandering or profiling.

Nowadays, state legislatures must be careful in how they draw up voting districts, especially in southern state legislatures. Because how many southern state legislatures abused their power in really suppressing minority citizen voters in the past, everybody now looks with a careful eye to avoid discriminatory voter intent. Quite frankly, I see no truth in any of the challenger's claims of these lawsuits. These types of indeed partisan gerrymandering do bring up a question of discriminatory intent. But if the legislatures are not denying the person's right to vote, there is no discriminatory intent.

Let me put this scenario for all Americans, if the Oregon state legislature decides to re-draw their voting districts maps and split one conservative district into two districts. Would you consider that a violation of the Equal Protection Clause or the electoral clauses? No, as long as their votes will not be denied, there is no violation. Actually, a legislature did officialized this plan and redrew the sixth congressional district of Maryland. The Maryland state legislature grabbed a

III. The Fifteenth Amendment, 1870

portion of the western part of Montgomery County, Maryland and added it to the sixth congressional district. Montgomery County is one the richest and yet most liberal counties on the Washington DC beltway and they grabbed a chunk of it and placed to a district that was fairly republican. Was that principled gerrymandering or partisan gerrymandering? In my opinion, it was partisan gerrymandering, and the state court should have stricken it due in part being unjustly gerrymandered.

What the Maryland state legislature did is what the legislatures of Florida, Texas, North Carolina, Louisiana, California are doing. Unjust political gerrymandering by playing these games against our Constitution. From using our established Electoral Clauses to play partisan political games and a possible Fifteenth Amendment violation.

This is the evils of a two-corrupt political party system trying to undermine our constitution and engaging in partisan power to control the reins of the national government. The idea of gerrymandering is not to bring it under a national governance. It is to do it in local control. But we have brought this nation under the depth of a massive dependency of national control, that we have forgotten our constitutional principles and brought it forth under partisanship tyranny. The curse of a two-party system.

Now the high court of the land is going to re-hear again, another case of gerrymandering proportion involving another lawsuit of partisan gerrymandering that may or may not consist of discriminatory intent...but the possibility is possible being in the sovereign state of Louisiana. The land of the famous populist corrupt individual Huey Long.

"These consolidated cases involve a constitutional challenge to Louisiana's most recent congressional districting map, Senate Bill 8 (SB8). The State passed SB8 in response

The Amendments

to a District Court order that required Louisiana to create an additional majority-black district to avoid "vote dilution" and comply with Section II of the VRA." (Dissenting Opinion of Louisiana, Appellant v. Phillipp Callais, 2025 by Associate Justice Clarence Thomas).

The great state of Louisiana is acting compassionately in creating an electoral law for them not to appear as the one unconstitutional racist as they were once. Now they are appearing to be the now unconstitutional bigots as the rest of the nation is pursuing to become.

As this union of sovereign states, after 1865 began to reshape into a republic of liberty and equality. It did not mean to continue to build it up on divisions. On party divisions, race divisions, or other unjust and unconstitutional divisions. When creating a white privilege division against other races, or minority privilege against the white races is a concept against the constitution. One is called racism, while the other is called reverse racism. Both are despicable and must be repudiated for the sanity of our American republic.

"Congress requires this Court to exercise jurisdiction over constitutional challenges to congressional redistricting, and we accordingly have an obligation to resolve such challenges promptly." (Dissenting Opinion of Louisiana, Appellant v. Phillipp Callais, 2025 by Associate Justice Clarence Thomas).

Congress does not require anybody to exercise anything to dictate an electoral law onto the states. To resolve such electoral law challenges should be resolved at the state level, preferably at the state legislature level, not the courts.

The national government leveled the playing fields within the constitution for the states to apply liberty and equality for all people residing in their respective states. It did not mean to play partisan politics or denying rights to some and showing privilege to a few.

III. The Fifteenth Amendment, 1870

This Louisiana state law and other state laws being created now is not what the constitutional framers were seeking from us to form a more perfect union. Let alone the Fifteenth Amendment framers to bring this union closer to liberty and equality.

D. Women's Right to Vote
Small Introduction to the Nineteenth Amendment

Section I: The right of citizens of the United States to vote shall not be denied or abridged by the United States or by any State on account of sex

Section II: Congress shall have power to enforce this article by appropriate legislation

Women has played a role in our American republic. From our establishment of our republic to later constitutional amendment changes to our republic. From the creation of our Star and Spangled banner by Betsy Ross to the nursing capabilities of Martha Washington. Then to the humanitarian and equal work of our American nurses of Dorothea Dix to other nurses venturing to care to mend our union's wounded soldiers during the civil war. Then to the hard work of our female citizens during the world wars, but that was after the induction of the nationwide Nineteenth Amendment's female's right to vote.

Am I a sexist? Many people have called me, "a sexist" due to the absolute reasoning that I oppose for the women to not have a nationalized electoral right. Nothing could be further from the truth. I do not oppose the American female citizenry in having a voice in public and community

III. The Fifteenth Amendment, 1870

service. I oppose then in having a national voting right to that female right.

I do not believe I am a sexist since I am a strong proponent of our American federalism republic of sovereign states to be abided by our federal constitution.

The key question to ask all around America, is if the female citizen of this American republic has ever been denied any part of their constitutional rights. As a member of the minority citizenry has been constantly denied their constitutional rights. The female citizen of this nation was never once discriminated or put in chains as other people has endured this cruel lifestyle.

The Fifteenth Amendment was created to satisfy the safety needs and protections of our citizens from not being denied their voting rights and privileges. Also, to make it known that no citizen should be discriminated on the account of race or color. Which I believe the Fifteenth Amendment covers both male and female persons of race and color their right to vote. One legal constitutional scholar would make the claim that this amendment could serve as a protection for all citizens, both male and female without the discrimination of race or color. It all depends how you wish to interpret the amendment's language, but quite honestly, I would say this amendment includes all citizens and there was not needed for another amendment creation in 1919 or later an Equal Rights Amendment in the middle of the twentieth century.

I cannot blame the female suffragette movement in wanting their own amendment for a national voting standard. But if people would read the Constitution with the newly added amendments...we would recognize that all Americans; male or female, black or white had voting rights. Political parties and movements are always trying to create political barriers and divisions rather than bring principled unity under federalism.

The Amendments

Eighteen sovereign states were granting suffrage rights to our American female citizens. From Washington state, Oregon, California, Nevada, Utah, Arizona, Colorado, Kansas, ARKANSAS, Wyoming, Idaho, Montana, North Dakota, Nebraska, Illinois, Indiana, Ohio, and Michigan. While sadly, twenty-five sovereign states were not granting suffrage rights to our American female citizens. From Maine, New Hampshire, Vermont, Rhode Island, Connecticut, New York, Pennsylvania, New Jersey, Delaware, Maryland, Virginia, West Virginia, North Carolina, South Carolina, Tennessee, Kentucky, Georgia, Alabama, Florida, Mississippi, Louisiana, Texas, Oklahoma, New Mexico, Minnesota, and South Dakota.

Female American citizens already have constitutional rights and when they added the Fifteenth Amendment, women as well as man of all race and color are included in this amendment. There truly was no need to establish an amendment based on sex...what is next an amendment stating that gender-binary people or transexual American individuals need a federal mandated voting rights amendment? No, the Fifteenth Amendment is quite clear, and we do not need to continue to create more barriers and divisions.

The Nineteenth Amendment was just a waste of federal government spending, just like the Eighteen Amendment outlawing the liquor production and consumption in the United States and its federal territories. Which coincidentally, it was the female suffragette movement that began the Temperance movement in favor of liquor prohibition. This same group was there to establish their own national voting rights standard. Minnesota, the home of Representative Andrew Volstead. The man who sponsored the liquor prohibition legislation that turned into the infamous Eighteen Amendment. His state was not granting women voting rights.

III. The Fifteenth Amendment, 1870

The hypocrisy of a movement just to gain a vote for one piece of legislation and deny it to others.

The Nineteenth Amendment did not have to take place in this American republic of sovereign states. It only occurred because the reshaped American republic began to increase its influence into a new largely and exuberant national style of governance against the principles of federalism.

Men, women, of all races are citizens of this republic are entitled to the right of vote bestowed by the Fifteenth Amendment. This nation was once divided but finally came to terms to that right to vote for all, with no sense of discrimination of privilege.

We are a republic of equality based for all as citizens: Male and female: Black; White, Hispanic, Asian, White-Indo-European, African, etc. And within these citizens, they have the right to vote. No government entity, federal and state can take it away for any reason except if justifiably committed criminal offense. A vote used to be an idea of privilege. But now it has become a right and therefore cannot be disparaged or denied. Once a right, especially voting is denied, we are no longer living in a representative republic but in an authoritarian democracy.

* * *

Our motto for this republic, "All Equal Under Law." That motto stands tall among other nations and unique because we have that motto stamped with the sense of the pursuit of liberty, fraternity, and happiness. Thank god we live in this reshaped American republic of sovereign states. For the glory to have been reshaped for the better, and not for the worst.

Bibliography

CHAPTER I

Against the Force Bill by John C. Calhoun, 15th & 16th February, 1833

The Great Speeches and Orations of Daniel Webster, With an Essay on Daniel Webster as a Master of English Style by Edwin P. Whipple, Daniel Webster. The Case of Gibbons and Ogden in the Supreme Court of the United States, February term, 1824.

Chief Justice Roger Taney, Ableman v. Booth, 1859.

Thomas W. Knox, Camp-Fire and Cotton-Field: Southern Adventure in Time of War: Life with the Union Armies, and Residence on a Louisiana Plantatio, New York: Blelock & Co., 1865; p. 317 Quoted in Daniel, "Metamorphosis of Slavery" (1979), pp. 89-90.

Race & Liberty in America, The Essential Reader, Edited by Jonathan Bean, The Independent Institute, The University Press of Kentucky, 2009.

Judah P. Benjamin, The Jewish Confederate, Eli N. Evans, The Free Press, a division of MacMillan, Inc., 1988

Slavery in the District of Columbia. Remarks made in the Senate of the United States, on the 10th of January 1838, upon a resolution moved by Mr. Clay as a substitute for the resolution offered by Mr. Calhoun on the subject of slavery in the District of Columbia

Bibliography

CHAPTER II

Opinion of the Court of the Slaughter-House Cases, 83 U.S. at 78, Associate Justice Samuel Freeman, 1873

Dissenting Opinion of the Court of the Slaughter-House Cases, 83 U.S. at 78, Associate Justice Noah H. Swayne, 1873

Opinion Brief of Plessy v. Ferguson, Associate Justice Henry Billings Brown

Dissenting Brief of Plessy v. Ferguson, Associate Justice John Marshall Harlan

Race & Liberty in America, The Essential Reader, Edited by Jonathan Bean, The Independent Institute, 2009, page 111

Opinion Brief of Buchanan v. Whaley, Associate Justice William R. Day

Race & Liberty in America, The Essential Reader, Edited by Jonathan Bean, The Independent Institute, The University Press of Kentucky, 2009.

Opinion Brief of Brown v. Board of Education, 1954, Chief Justice Earl Warren

Oral Argument of John W. Davis, Esq., on behalf of Appellees R.W. Elliot et al., Brown v. Board of Education, 1954

Oral Argument Question of Associate Justice Robert Jackson on R.W. Elliot et al., Brown v. Board of Education, 1954

Syllabus of Richmond v. J.A. Croson Co ruling, 1989

Dissenting Opinion of Richmond v. J.A. Croson Co ruling, Associate Justice Thurgood Marshall, 1989

The Conscience of a Conservative, Goldwater, Barry M., Regnery Gateway, 1990

Foundations of the Republic, Equality of Rights, Calvin Coolidge, University of the Press of the Pacific, Honolulu, Hawaii, p. 72.

The Amendments

Foundations of the Republic, Toleration and Liberalism, Calvin Coolidge, University of the Press of the Pacific, Honolulu, Hawaii, p. 299-300.
Opinion of the Court of United States v. Virginia, by Associate Justice Ruth B. Ginsburg, 1996
Dissenting Opinion of the Court of United States v. Virginia, by Associate Justice Antonin Scalia, 1996
Opinion of Richmond v. J.A. Croson Co ruling, Associate Justice Sandra Day O'Connor, 1989
Concurrence Opinion of Richmond v. J.A. Croson Co ruling, Associate Justice Antonin Scalia, 1989
Opinion of Bowers v. Hardwick, Associate Justice Byron White, 1984
The Making of a Justice: Reflections on My First 94 Years, Justice Paul Stevens, Little Brown and Company, 2019. Dissenting Opinion of Bowers v. Hardwick, by Associate Justice John Paul Stevens p. 405
Concurring Opinion of Bowers v. Hardwick, Chief Justice Warren Burger, 1984
Concurrence Opinion of Bowers v. Hardwick, Associate Justice Lewis Powell, 1984)
Majority Opinion of Loving v. Virginia, Chief Justice Earl Warren, 1967
Scalia's Court, Kevin A. Ring, 2004, 2016
Concurring Opinion of Plyler v. Doe, Associate Justice Harry Blackmun, 1982
Opinion of Lawrence v. Texas, 2003 by Associate Justice Anthony Kennedy
Dissenting Opinion of Lawrence v. Texas, 2003 by Associate Justice Clarence Thomas
Opinion Brief on Planned Parenthood SE PA v. Casey, Associate Justice Sandra Day O'Connor, 1992

Bibliography

Dissenting Brief on Planned Parenthood SE PA v. Casey, Chief Justice William Rehnquist, 1992

Opinion Brief of Buck v. Bell, 1927 by Associate Justice Oliver Wendell Holmes

Opinion Brief of Roe v. Wade by Associate Justice Harry Blackmun, 1973

Dissenting Brief of *Roe v. Wade* by Associate Justice Richard Rehnquist, 1973

Dissenting Brief on Planned Parenthood SE PA v. Casey, Chief Justice William Rehnquist, 1992

Syllabus of Dobbs v. Jackson Women's Health Organization, 2022

Opinion Brief of Dobbs v. Jackson Women's Health Organization, Associate Justice Samuel Alito, 2022

Donald J. Trump v. Norma Anderson, 2024, Oral Argument of Jonathan F. Mitchell, Petitioner

Dissenting opinion of Vance v. Terrazas, 1980 by Associate Justice William Brennan

Opinion Brief of Saenz v. Roe, 1999 by Associate Justice John Paul Stevens

The Making of a Justice: Reflections on My First 94 Years, Justice Paul Stevens, Little Brown and Company, 2019

Concurring Opinion of *INS v. Cardoza-Fonseca* by Associate Justice Antonin Scalia, 1987

Opinion Brief of Donald J. Trump, President of the United States, Et At., Petitioners v. Hawaii by Chief Justice John Roberts, 2018

Dissenting Brief of Donald J. Trump, President of the United States, Et At., Petitioners v. Hawaii by Associate Justice Sonia Sotomayor, 2018

Oral Argument of Trump v. CASA, Incorporated, and consolidated cases, by Solicitor General D. John Sauer, 2025

The Amendments

Born in the U.S.A.? Rethinking Birthright Citizenship in the Wake of 9/11, Eastman, C., John, Chapman University School of Law, 2008

Oral Argument of Trump v. CASA, Incorporated, and consolidated cases, Question by Associate Justice Sonia Sotomayor, 2025

Oral Argument of Trump v. CASA, Incorporated, and consolidated cases, Question by Associate Justice Amy Coney Barrett, 2025

Opinion of the Court of Trump v. CASA, Inc., by Associate Justice Amy Coney Barrett, 2025

Dissenting Opinion of the Court of Trump v. CASA, Inc., by Associate Justice Ketanji Brown Jackson, 2025

Concurring Opinion of the Court of Trump v. Hawaii, by Associate Justice Clarence Thomas, 2018

Syllabus Brief of United States, Petitioner v. Jonathan Skrmetti, Attorney General and Reporter for Tennessee, 2025

Opinion Brief of United States, Petitioner v. Jonathan Skrmetti, Attorney General and Reporter for Tennessee, by Chief Justice John Roberts, 2025

Concurring Brief of United States, Petitioner v. Jonathan Skrmetti, Attorney General and Reporter for Tennessee, by Associate Justice Amy Coney Barrett, 2025

Dissenting Brief of United States, Petitioner v. Jonathan Skrmetti, Attorney General and Reporter for Tennessee, by Associate Justice Sonia Sotomayor, 2025

CHAPTER III

Opinion Brief of Giles v. Harris, by Associate Justice Oliver Wendell Holmes, 1903

The Debates in the Several States Conventions, vol. 3, James Madison

Bibliography

Dissenting Opinion of Arizona State Legislature v. Arizona Independent Redistricting Commission, by Associate Justice Antonin Scalia, 2015

Oral Argument of Mr. Neal K. Katyal, on behalf of the respondents on Moore v. Harper, December 7, 2022

Dissenting Opinion on Mark Brnovivh, Attorney General of Arizona, Et Al., Petitioners v. Democratic National Committee, Et Al. by Associate Justice Elena Kagan, 2021

Opinion Brief on Mark Brnovivh, Attorney General of Arizona, Et Al., Petitioners v. Democratic National Committee, Et Al. by Associate Justice Samuel Alito, 2021

Report of the Comm'n on Fed. Election Reform, Building Confidence in U.S. Elections 46 (Sept. 2005)

Judgment syllabus of Moore v. Harper, 2023

Opinion of the Court for Moore v. Harper, 2023 by Chief Justice John Roberts

Concurring Opinion of the Court for Moore v. Harper, 2023 by Associate Justice Brett Kavanaugh

Concurring Opinion by Associate Justice C. Thomas for Alexander, President of the South Carolina Senate v. South Carolina State Conference of the NAACP, 2024

Dissenting Opinion by Associate Justice E. Kagan for Alexander, President of the South Carolina Senate v. South Carolina State Conference of the NAACP, 2024

Opinion Brief by Chief Justice John Roberts for Rucho v. Common Cause, 2019

Dissenting Opinion of Louisiana, Appellant v. Phillipp Callais, 2025 by Associate Justice Clarence Thomas

LISTEN ON SPREAKER, SPOTIFY, I ♥ RADIO, GOOGLE PODCASTS STATES RIGHTS RADIO

E-Mail: statesrightsradio@mail.com
Instagram: state.rights.radio

www.ingramcontent.com/pod-product-compliance
Lightning Source LLC
Chambersburg PA
CBHW020338010526
44119CB00035B/451/J